ROBERT BILLINGS COLE

An American Life

Copyright © 2023
First Edition
All right reserved

ISBN: 9798392004775
Independently published

Autobiography by Robert Billings Cole,
with the collaboration of Gary Horstkorta,
and with the relentless proofreading by Jennifer Heinschel –
daughter of Robert Billings Cole.

Photos from Robert Billings Cole collection – unless otherwise noted
Book design by Doris Walker, Comp Graphic, Sandpoint, Idaho

Cover: Leprechaun Green

TO ELLEN:

"You are my Sunshine"

TABLE OF CONTENTS

- Preface 7
- Introduction 9
- Chapter One – Family Background 11
- Chapter Two – Cars First, Girls Second 31
- Chapter Three – Sports Cars & ROTC 39
- Chapter Four – Go West Young Man 47
- Chapter Five – Change Of Direction 57
- Chapter Six – Racing & New Opportunities 73
- Chapter Seven – On My Own 85
- Chapter Eight – The Candy Store Story 101
- Chapter Nine – Collector Cars 113
- Chapter Ten – Pebble Beach 151
- Chapter Eleven – Big Boat Sailing 173
- Chapter Twelve – Reflections 205
- Appendix One – Adages, Idioms & Axioms 228
- Appendix Two – Time Line 234
- Many Thanks 238
- Final Word 241

PREFACE

Over the years I read or heard several phrases or adages that I particularly liked and took to heart. I have thought about or used them often, so they became part of my daily approach to life. Of these, three are the most meaningful to me:

- Press on Regardless — This phrase captured my attention as a young man and became part of my approach to life and career. Perhaps it was our country's response to the events of World War II or just my own drive and initiative that motivated me to adopt the phrase as my life's mantra. From an early age, regardless of whatever difficult situations I found myself involved in, I would "press on" until I found a solution. Along with a positive attitude, determination, and the ability to surround myself with good friends and associates, I was able to succeed in most endeavors I embarked on whether it be in college, the military, sports, road racing, sailing, or business.

- Do not go where the path may lead. Go instead where there is no path and leave a trail. **~ From Ralph Waldo Emerson**

- It always seemed strange to me, the things we admire in men — kindness and generosity — openness and honesty — understanding and feeling — are the concomitants of failure in our system; and those we detest — sharpness, greed, acquisitiveness, meanness, egotism, and self-interest — are the traits of success — while men admire the quality of the first, they love the product of the second. **~ From John Steinbeck**

INTRODUCTION

From time to time over the past several years, many of my friends have asked me to write a book about my life, but perhaps I have been too busy suffering the slings and arrows of advancing old age to undertake the project. However, over the last couple of years, I have had the time to think more about my past activities and events I have created and been involved in. Looking through my photo albums helped jog my memory about my earliest years since some of those photographs go back over 100 years.

There are three primary areas of my life which I have chronicled in some detail in this book – sports car road racing, my involvement with collector cars, and big boat sailing. These parts of my life overlapped at some point which kept me quite busy for many years. Throughout this journey, I have been fortunate to meet and become friends with many wonderful people who helped and encouraged me to undertake new endeavors. Much of my success is a result of key people who played important roles in my life, many of whom you will meet in the following pages.

It has been a great ride, and this opportunity to recall so many memories has been a very enjoyable experience. Perhaps you will learn a few new things about Bob Cole you were not aware of, but in any case, I hope you enjoy the book.

PRESS ON!

BOB COLE

Me at six years old with my paternal grandmother, grandfather, and mother (R), in 1938

Christmas with my father, brother Jim, me, sister Beverly, and my mother at home in Evanston, Illinois, 1934

Press On... Regardless!

– CHAPTER ONE –
FAMILY BACKGROUND

Like many 19th-century families, my parents' family trees reveal a familiar path of immigration from overseas to the United States, eventually settling in the Midwest. My great-grandparents immigrated from Ireland, England, and Scotland, and settled in Ontario, Canada, where my grandfather was born in 1865 in the town of Dawn Mills. Although born a Canuck, he left Dawn Mills in 1889 and made his way to St. Joseph, Missouri, where my father, James Albert Cole Sr., was born on December 17, 1890. I recall my brother, Jim, telling me about a newspaper article in the St. Joseph, Missouri, newspaper regarding our great-grandfather making a trip from Ontario, Canada, to visit his son in St. Joseph. He was 104 years old at the time (born in 1830). When he passed away at 109, he was believed to have been the oldest person in America.

My mother's mother and father immigrated to the United States from Scotland and Ireland, respectively. My mother, Alice Clara (Heafey) Flanagan, was born on August 5, 1899, in Omaha, Nebraska. Interestingly, her father's cousin was Edward Flanagan of Ireland. He arrived in the United States in 1904 and, after being ordained a priest in 1912, became better known as Father Flanagan. He established Father Flanagan's Boys Home in Omaha, later to become known simply as Boys Town, which is still in operation today and is a National Historic Landmark in Nebraska.

After marrying in 1921, my father and mother moved from Omaha to Evanston, Illinois, where I was born in 1932. My father, in his early 40s, accepted a position as the Senior Vice President of Nye, Schneider and Jenks, the largest grain company in the world, so after a short time in Evanston, we moved to Edina, Minnesota. When the Depression set in and the grain company failed due to the prolifagacy of the owners, my father helped form a grain co-op, an effort that was noticed by certain people in the U.S. Department of Agriculture. As a result, he was asked to go to Washington D.C.

My father at his desk in Minneapolis working as Director of the Commodity Credit Corporation – U.S. Department of Agriculture

along with Jesse Tapp, the then President of Bank of America. As part of President Roosevelt's New Deal Program, together they were the architects of the Farm Parity Program including the Commodity Stabilization Service (CSS) and the Commodity Credit Corporation (CCC) in the late 1930s for the U.S. Government.

With the job change, the family had moved to Chevy Chase, Maryland, for the duration of my father's work. In his job, my father had regular contact with many of the politicians in Congress. This led to an invitation for my parents and me to attend the annual White House Easter Egg Hunt on two occasions. I was about six or seven years old at the time.

When his job concluded in 1939, the Department of Agriculture offered him a high-level position managing all the U.S. grain concerns outside the country. However, despite the importance of the position, he declined the offer because it would have required a move to London, England. This proved to be a wise decision considering the onset of World War II was close at hand and London would soon be under siege. Instead, my father took a position as Director of the CCC and CSS for the U.S. Department of Agriculture in its largest office outside of Washington D.C. The office was in Minneapolis – home of the grain giants General Mills, Cargill, and Archer, Daniels, Midland. The family returned to Minneapolis to settle down just as war broke out in Europe. This was a pretty remarkable career path considering my father was still a young man in his 40s.

A TALENTED FAMILY

I have two older siblings – my sister, Beverly, who was born in 1923, and my brother, Jim, who was born in 1927. Beverly was very intelligent and showed exceptional talent for playing the piano early on, so my mother made sure she received proper instruction. As she progressed, Beverly became a very talented musician. Listening to her practice on our Steinway piano, I decided to give it a try. While I appreciated her music, I preferred to take contemporary songs and put them to a Boogie Woogie beat and, with practice, I became a good player. I continued playing for many years and, along with Boogie Woogie (Albert Ammons, Meade Lux Lewis, Pete Johnson), taught myself to play classical music including excerpts from original scores by Beethoven, Chopin, and Mozart, plus George Shearing and Dave Brubeck.

Beverly won scholarships in piano to the Juilliard School and then The Philadelphia Conservatory of Music. Her instructor at both schools was the renowned Olga Samaroff Stokowski (Leopold

Beverly in 1962

Beverly practicing on her organ at home in later years

Chapter 1 – Family Background • 13

Beverly with husband Bill Tarbell outside their home in Minneapolis

Playing the piano was one of my favorite activities which I learned at home on the Steinway parlor grand piano shown here. Listening in is my niece Marta. Photo taken in 1961

Stokowski's wife). Beverly went on to become a concert pianist for the Washington Symphony Orchestra, played at Carnegie Hall, and became the organist and Minister of Music for the Hennepin Avenue Methodist Church in Minneapolis. As the organist, Beverly played the second largest pipe organ in the U.S., and her selections included the five Bach Fugues which she had memorized and played for the public. She also earned two Master's degrees in music and Spanish.

One of Beverly's acquaintances, and fellow student of Stokowki's, was William Kapell, a world-renowned classical pianist and one of only three musicians signed by RCA Victor as a "Red Seal Artist" (the other two were violinist Jascha Heifetz and pianist Vladimir Horowitz). When Kapell, then only in his early 20s, traveled to Minneapolis for a concert, he would come to our house to practice on Beverly's Steinway piano. Kapell especially favored women with red hair and Beverly, of Irish decent, had red hair which enhanced the attraction. He eventually proposed to her, but she turned him down since she was waiting for her true love to return from his military tour in Europe.

I couldn't believe that anyone could play the piano the way Kapell did; it was incredible. Our family would attend his local performances with the Minneapolis Symphony Orchestra conducted by Antal Dorati, then go backstage for the post-concert gathering. Unfortunately, Kapell died in a plane crash in California's Santa Cruz Mountains returning from a tour of Australia in 1953 — a tragic loss.

Beverly married a World War II Army Air Corps veteran, Carl Schmidt, who had flown many tours as a crew member in B-17s in Europe. He was a "triple threat man" — navigator, bombardier, and radar operator, plus one of the first to use the Norden Bombsight. He was a really neat guy and he brought home with him a little British Austin sedan that he let me drive. What a great little car. I was quite enamored with it. His father was the head of the medical school at the University of Pennsylvania, so Carl and Beverly moved to Levittown near Philadelphia. They had one child, a daughter Marta, who went on to earn a degree at the University of Minnesota, continuing the family tradition. Beverly eventually divorced and remarried a very nice fellow, Bill Tarbell, who was head of the engineering school at 3M in Minneapolis.

When my brother, James Albert Cole Jr., graduated second in his class from a military high school, he was awarded the number one assignment in Minnesota to the West Point Academy. Unfortunately, he could not pass the physical exam

Family gathering in 1957, me and brother Jim in back, my mother, sister Beverly, my father and niece Marta

Chapter 1 — Family Background • 15

My father and mother were dedicated travelers in retirement

due to astigmatism. Instead, at 19 years old, he enrolled at the University of Minnesota and spent two years there before enlisting in the Army Officers Candidate School (OCS) where he received his commission as second Lieutenant and was assigned to Army Intelligence. He served his tour of duty with the U.S. Occupation Forces in post-war Germany. While still in Germany, he sent home two German Shepherd dogs, Axel and Alex, for me to look after until he returned.

Even though Jim was a very accomplished singer, he did not pursue a musical career. While in Germany, he studied opera with Gerhard Husch, a renowned German opera singer, and when visiting us once in Minnesota, Jim surprised us with a beautiful rendition of an aria. Occasionally during our family gatherings, we would listen to recorded music and Jim would stand up and would act as the conductor of the orchestra, not missing a beat. After his military service ended, he returned to the University of Minnesota and earned a degree in Economics. He eventually married, became a stockbroker with Paine Webber, and moved to California in the late 1960s.

As the youngest member in my family, I trailed behind my sister and brother to attend local schools from first grade all the way through high school in Minneapolis. I enrolled at the University of Minnesota majoring in Psychology with a minor in Air, Science, and Tactics, but I had an inauspicious first semester. Instead of paying attention to my studies, I "majored" in sharpening my pool skills, playing Boogie Woogie on the piano at parties, and enjoying the college atmosphere. This led to academic probation which certainly got my attention and set me back on the right track. I didn't arrive at the real world until my senior year, but more about my college adventures follows in the next few chapters.

My father continued working until he was 70 years old, receiving congressional approval to go beyond the "mandatory" retirement age of 65 due to his experience and value to the Department of Agriculture. When he did retire, he was rewarded with a bronze plaque and a month-long trip to Europe, which included tickets to the 1960 Summer Olympic Games in Rome.

He and my mother moved to a Del Webb retirement community in Arizona and spent a good part of their time traveling all over the United States, Mexico, and Canada towing a small house trailer wherever they went.

With both of my parents being born in the 1890s, they were immensely proud of their three children, all of whom graduated from college with their daughter becoming a highly skilled concert pianist and both sons becoming military officers.

Chapter 1 – Family Background • 17

ELLEN

Of course, I have had a forever partner along the way. Ellen – world rank superstar – the personification of NICE! Undeterred by my individualism, she saved my emotional life with her constant love and affection. I couldn't be more grateful. With the greenest of thumbs and world-class cooking skills, she tends her gardens, our home, and me without (serious) complaint and is always putting others in the forefront of her every thought and activity. It has been a joy to be her partner for more than 50 years. She is certainly my "sunshine."

I first met Ellen late in 1969 near the San Francisco Yacht Harbor. I was pulling into a parking place from a luncheon meeting in Sausalito with my CPA, Del Begg, and my then business partner Frank Gyorgy, to pick up my car (Lotus Elan 2+2) parked near my boat at the yacht harbor. At that time, boat owners were allowed to park off Marina Boulevard near the walking path close to their slips. As I was pulling into the parking lot, I noticed a gorgeous young woman standing near the rock wall near my car. She was obviously in distress, and I quickly noticed a Volkswagen Beetle stopped in one of the two lanes on Marina Boulevard. This was during rush hour, so there was a line of cars backed up for blocks behind the VW trying to get past.

"Is that your car?" I asked. "What happened?" She told me the car had just stopped running. She already called AAA but didn't know when they were going to arrive. I told her I'd take a look at her car, and saw the coil wire had fallen off the coil. I immediately reattached it and said to her, "We had better get in the car because if it starts, we are out of here." You certainly could not make such a simple fix with a complex modern car! I intentionally drove around for a while to confirm the car was running properly and to get to know this very pleasant, gorgeous creature better. Eventually I pulled into a Standard Gas Station to make a visual check on the coil and wire. All was good so we drove back to the yacht harbor where my car was parked, and I made sure that before I got out of the car, I got her phone number.

Ellen lived in Sausalito in a very small apartment on one of those steep hills. One day I arrived for a visit and found she and her father had arranged to have an upright piano moved into the

Ellen and I made a 50th anniversary visit to the spot where we first met in 1969

Ellen and me behind the plaque dedicated to James Cole Hill (unknown if a relative) at Plymouth, Conn., and across the road from a "waterline" replica of the U.S.S. Constitution

apartment. I was still playing the piano, so one day I brought over some sheet music and played for her. We decided to move in together and found a two-story townhouse on the water next to what was to become the ferry dock in Sausalito. Since Ellen worked in the Ferry Building in San Francisco as an executive secretary, she only had to walk out the door and catch the ferry to her office in San Francisco.

We stayed in the town house for two years (1971-72), then in 1973 we moved to Hillsborough and were married in Virginia City, Nevada, at the Iron Door Saloon. We had decided to travel to Carson City to get a marriage license. After flying to Reno and renting a car, we were headed to Carson City when we saw a sign for Virginia City. On a lark, we decided to go visit that historic town. We stopped at Ed and Dottie Blankenship's saloon, the Iron Door, and engaged them in a conversation and told them about getting married. They told us where to find the county clerk to issue a license on her ranch outside of town. She provided us a marriage license, then directed us back into town to find the Justice of the

Chapter 1 – Family Background • **19**

Peace at the Bucket of Blood Saloon. We found this fellow who turned out to be quite a character – and drunk – then moved to the Iron Door and were married right in front of the restroom! After he performed the wedding ceremony, he would not take any payment except for a bottle of Jack Daniels which we duly bought and presented to him for his service.

In 1985, we moved out of our home in Hillsborough to a wonderful location on a hill in Woodside just off Highway 280. The home was built in 1916 and has a sweeping view to the east of the Bay Area. We subsequently named our home "Cole's Knoll," and have lived there for the past 38 years.

OUR FAMILY

I get a great deal of enjoyment being with Ellen and the rest of my family. Daughter Cari lives in New York City and owns a well-respected and successful voice school for the entertainment industry (caricole.com). Son Rob and his wife, Julie, live in Shingle Springs, California, and have two children, Lily and Aidan. Rob

Family gathering for my mother's 90th birthday
Back row: me, son Rob, brother-in-law Bill, brother Jim; middle row: wife Ellen, sister Beverly, daughter Cari; bottom row: daughter Jennifer, my mother, and daughter Kimberely

is the manager of a farm and a consultant on matters concerning the new world of regenerative farming. Daughter Kimberely, her husband, Alonzo (a member of Los Californios – Hispanic settlers of California), and daughters Ruby and Honora live in Eureka, California. Kimberely is a mentor and healer for personal growth and well-being and founder of Unshakable Soul (unshakablesoul.com). Daughter Jennifer, her husband, Joel (the production manager at Children's Musical Theater, San Jose), and children Colette and Kies live nearby in Redwood City, California. Jennifer is a veteran elementary-school teacher, teaching 3rd and 4th grade for 20 years.

– CHAPTER ONE –
PHOTO GALLERY

My dad (R) in 1918 aboard the training ship U.S.S Pennsylvania

My father, taken in 1914, sitting in his boat, The Arrow, which he built

Evanston, Illinois, in 1931. My parents' and my first home. I was born in 1932

My dad with friends in The Arrow, a wooden boat he built

My dad standing next to his first car

My father and sister Beverly standing next to our family car. Taken in 1926

Family reunion in the 1930s in St. Joseph, Missouri

Chapter 1 – Family Background • **23**

With my dad in 1935

My mother, me, and our 1935 Oldsmobile

1936 – Riding a three wheeler

Ellen and me on our 10th anniversary. Photo by Roy Dryer taken in 1983

1939 – My father built this soap box derby racer for my brother, Jim, but we both used it

Father and Mother panning for gold in Alaska in 1966

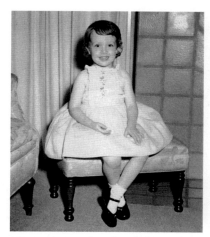

Niece Marta, daughter of my sister, Beverly, circa 1957

Daughter Kimberely entertaining us at six years old

This was an ad for new newspaper subscriptions with me in the photo

My trusty bicycle which I used on my paper route. I am about 13 years old

My father and me

Photo taken of my dad in his office with the plaque that sat on his desk

26 • *Press On... Regardless!*

Sister Beverly and me in the 1980s

Daughter Jennifer adjusts my tie prior to the annual St. Francis Yacht Club Father Daughter Dance in 1983

With daughter Cari and my 1957 Lotus Elite

Chapter 1 – Family Background • 27

My son Rob and me with then-newest member of our family. Three generations of Coles

---

WALTER H. JUDD
5TH DIST. MINNESOTA

COMMITTEES:
INSULAR AFFAIRS
EDUCATION

Congress of the United States
House of Representatives
Washington, D. C.

September 15, 1945

AIR MAIL

Mr. James Albert Cole, Jr.
5003 1st Avenue South
Minneapolis, Minnesota

Dear James:

    Just a note to advise you that I am able to give you an appointment as principal for one of my two vacancies in the Military Academy, providing the physical examination is satisfactory. If the War Department has not sent you instructions, as it is supposed to, please send me a wire and I will prod it a little. It is so swamped these days with the work of demobilization that it may have slipped up on this item.

    I know you and your parents and friends were anxious to know your final standing and will be glad at the result.

Sincerely yours,

Walter H. Judd

---

28 • *Press On... Regardless!*

This 1931 Pontiac Split Head 6 was my first car for all of $50.00, friend Bob Carlson at the wheel

My spiffy 1941 Plymouth Club coupe. Note the headlight covers, required during World War II blackouts

Press On... Regardless!

– CHAPTER TWO –

CARS FIRST, GIRLS SECOND

Moving into my teenage years and high school brought about happy times and several memorable moments. One such moment would unknowingly change my life and point me towards a career I had not yet envisioned or considered. Like most teenage boys who turn 16 years of age, I couldn't wait to get my driver's license and my first car.

Before I received my license, my mother took me out near the Wold-Chamberlain Minneapolis Airport and taught me how to drive. Using our 1939 Buick Four Door Sedan Special, we would drive up and down those country roads until I learned enough to take the driving test. I passed the test and now with a license, all I needed was a car.

With my father's help, my buddy Bob Carlson (later an Eagle Scout and I got a summer job with the U.S. Forestry Department in Grand Marais, which is in the northern part of Minnesota, not far from the Canadian border. We were in a camp with about 10 or 15 others and our job was to walk through the forest of white pine trees looking for a specific bush, called the Ribey Bush, which was infecting the trees. We would spread lime on the bush to kill it and save the trees. Since we were away from the camp, we would pack a lunch and throw it over a tree branch to keep it away from the bears.

We heard of this car for sale 10 or 15 miles south of Grand Marais near Lake Superior in a logging camp back off the highway. The car was available for $50, so we came up with the money, and Bob and I decided to look at the car. We had somebody drive us to the camp and upon arrival, out came this big strapping fellow to talk with us.

The car, a 1931 Pontiac Split Head 6, had semi-truck snap ring wheels and tires. The logger had us climb into the car, then he cranked the engine over with the hand crank and it started. We gave him the money and off we went. On our way out to the highway, I discovered the brakes didn't work, which turned out to be just the beginning of the car's problems.

I insisted on driving the car to the highway when the lack of brakes caused us a real problem. As we approached Highway 61, we had to negotiate a 110-degree turn, so I grabbed the emergency brake, turned the steering wheel and the car made the turn, on two wheels, onto the highway. The lights went out and the engine stopped, so we pushed the car off to the side of the road and were able to flag down an approaching car using our Zippo lighters. Mind you, there was very little to no traffic on the roads, so we were fortunate when a car came along.

The driver said there was a gas station not far away, so he pushed our car with his to the gas station. We gassed up with the engine running and drove along the Gunflint Trail back to our camp – all of this at night. On the narrow dirt road into our camp, the lights went out again, so we had wait for other cars to come by so we could follow them using their headlights. We motored along for a few miles until the engine quit again. We pushed the car to the side of the road and hiked the rest of the way into camp. It was a pitch black night so every sound we heard raised the hair on the back of our neck. The next day we received a ride to our car, got it started, and drove it back to camp. Adventures of city boys in the country.

We used the car for a couple of months on weekends for trips around the area, but eventually it was time to head home and get ready for the school year. Just south of Duluth, we had a flat tire and since the car had big truck wheels and tires, we didn't have the tools to fix the tire. Once again, we pushed it off to the side of the road and hitchhiked home. We left the car there for a month until we decided to retrieve it. My dad gave us a ride up to the car's location and when he got out, he looked the car over. He walked up to the car, poked his finger right through a section of a rusted fender, said, "Pie crust," and shook his head. We brought some tools with us, removed the tire and had it repaired at a local gas station. We drove the car home and put it in my friend's garage with the intent of fixing all the little problems. Over the winter we took care of the problems as best we could. However, we couldn't get it started and there were many parts left over, so our parents had it towed to the junkyard.

Not dismayed with the first car ownership experience and still in high school, I continued my involvement with cars. I successively bought several different models, improved each one, then sold them and made a little money on each transaction. These included the following:

- 1936 Chevrolet two-door sedan
- 1948 Ford convertible (bought with my brother)
- 1941 Plymouth coupe
- 1948 Buick Four-Door Special slant-back

While enjoying my car hobby in high school, I also participated in school sports, especially tennis. I learned to play with my brother and his friends, all of whom were five years older than me. When we played together, they took no mercy on the new kid, so I had to learn fast!

Just so happens, my homeroom teacher was the tennis team coach, so after I beat his number one player in a tournament, I became his number two player during my junior and senior years. Ironically, I never beat that number one player again. Our high school team won two city championships plus, in state doubles team competition, a friend and I attained the semi-finals one year and the finals the next year.

After graduating from high school and enrolling at the University of Minnesota, I made my final acquisition of an American car – a 1941 Ford two-door sedan. I purchased the car with all my savings plus money earned from a variety of jobs during the summers – working in a bowling alley, bagging groceries, a paper route, and a job at W. R. Stevens Buick dealership. They assigned me to the Servi-Car, which was a three-wheel motorcycle. I would ride out to a customer's location, hitch it to their car, then drive the car to the dealership for service.

With the money earned, I embarked on a rebuild of my Ford's engine plus added several accessories to really make it my car. One of the mechanics at the Buick dealership told me when I first started the engine, I should drive the car for 50 miles without turning the engine off to break it in. I completed the journey with the engine running somewhat rough; turns out I had two of the spark plug wires reversed. I was quite proud of the Ford and drove it on a

My pride and joy, a 1941 Ford two-door sedan

daily basis and took very good care of it. I found it easier to attract girls if you had a cool car.

Also during my freshman and sophomore years at U of M, I had a couple of experiences that changed my attitude about college. Like high school, I thought college would be relatively easy, so I spent more time shooting pool and playing Boogie Woogie on the piano than I did on academics. It didn't take long before I was on academic probation as "real life" caught up with me. I had to refocus on my studies, eliminate pool from my personal activities, and minimize my piano pursuit.

During my freshman year, U of M had a talent show which I participated in. I played the piano and had the opportunity to share the stage with a drummer and a future international star — Gene Krupa. I also played at our fraternity house socials and other campus functions.

One of our more popular means of entertainment was the campus radio station, WMMR. My friend Jim Lange, a fraternity brother and later TV host of The Dating Game, got me a job at the station as a disc jockey. I remember the building was directly opposite the dormitory for female students. At night I would ask them to blink their room lights if they were listening to the station and when the lights came on, at least I knew someone out there was tuned in. Jim Lange and I would meet up again a few years later in San Francisco where he was a popular radio and TV host, and I sold him a Triumph sports car while working for Triumph in San Francisco.

While cars occupied a fair amount of my spare time (my motto was "cars first, girls second"), I remained active in sports through my fraternity. I played on my fraternity's intramural basketball team where I earned the nickname of "Uncie," short for unconscious, which is how my teammates described my unorthodox shots that somehow went in the basket. Our team was loaded with star athletes including Del May (All State Wisconsin in three sports in high school), brothers Bob and Pinky McNamara (both All-American football players), and Dick Dougherty (All-American hockey player). We won the intramural championship two years in a row, which was quite a feat since there were 27 fraternities at U of M.

THE AWAKENING

While still in college, one of my friends who was keen on cars suggested I go see the new model import sports cars at a local dealer. Intrigued, I drove to Archie Walker's (scion of the Walker Family) Imported Cars location (with the homecoming queen as my passenger), I walked into the showroom, and my world changed when I saw my very first MG TD. I remember the moment, I took

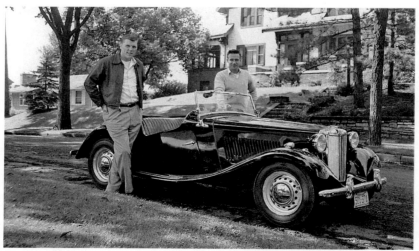

My first sports car. My good friend Del May on the left was all-state in baseball, basketball, and football. He was the center on our basketball team that won the U of M intramural championship. With a first name of Del, his pet dog was a Dalmatian of course

Chapter 2 – Cars First, Girls Second • **35**

My father seated in the MG TD

one look at the TD and fell in love...I couldn't believe what I was seeing. That moment is still indelibly etched in my mind. I took it for a test drive and knew I had to have one. Within a few days, I quit my job at the Buick Dealership and bugged the sports car dealer until they gave me a job as a gofer. I painted the parts department, the showroom, and any other job they wanted me to do.

I saved the money I earned to hopefully buy an MG until one day when good fortune came my way. An MG TD came into the dealership on a repossession, whatever that was. Expressing interest in the car to Jim Elliott, the General Manager, he worked out a time-payment program I could afford and just like that, I now had my first British sports car. This was late 1953, and little did I know this first MG was the beginning of a seven-decade long association with British cars. Of course, the 1941 Ford was quickly sold, and I began to explore the joys of owning a completely new type of car, unlike anything I had ever experienced before.

I received my first ticket in the TD for speeding on the Minnehaha Parkway. The officer told me he had tracked me on radar going over the speed limit. Radar...what the hell was radar? I didn't have the money to pay the fine, so I made my one phone call to my fraternity to have someone come bail me out. When the laughing stopped, they came to pay the fine, but I never heard the end of that little episode.

A large gathering of entrants at my first competition in the MG in 1954, a gymkhana field event, where car control is key

Press On... Regardless!

– CHAPTER THREE –
SPORTS CARS & ROTC

From the moment I bought the MG, I found more new friends who also owned sports cars. As a result, a good portion of my leisure time was occupied with these friends participating in various sports car activities. The group introduced me to the Land O'Lakes Region of the Sports Car Club of America (SCCA) with whom I became a member and entered my first event, a gymkhana, in September of 1954. Not a speed event, a gymkhana is more of a low key, skill contest held on an open field. A course is laid out on the field including turns and other maneuvers marked with sticks or cones plus a start and finish line. The object is to navigate the course in the shortest time without knocking over any of the markers. These events were a great way to meet other club members, have some fun, and learn more about car control.

For a rookie, I did well in these events and was eager to participate in other club activities including rallies and social gatherings. When a friend of mine, Don Skogmo (scion of the Gamble-Skogmo store chain), suggested I try ice racing, I didn't quite know what this activity entailed, but was curious. Don was a racer who owned several race cars including a new Jaguar D-Type which he kept at his custom-built home with a 12-car garage! Don owned a gas station, so I took my MG there to prepare it for the race. We readjusted the valves, put on a straight exhaust pipe, reduced the tire air pressures, and changed the oil. Then it was off to frozen Lake Phalen in nearby St. Paul. The club plowed the snow off the ice, then used a flame thrower borrowed from the military to melt the ice and spread sand on the surface around the course for traction. I had to take a driving test and they assigned me an instructor by the name of Russ Lee who just happened to be the Minnesota State dirt track champion. He got behind the wheel of my MG and proceeded to race the car around the ice track with the engine running at a very high RPM. I thought it would surely

Easy, keep the car between the sticks

break under such treatment. He told me the real trick to ice racing was to avoid hitting the snowbanks (good idea!) and not race down low but stay up on the high side away from the other cars to avoid their loss of traction as the sand wore away. I passed the test, entered the event, and, adhering to Lee's advice of staying on the high line, ended up winning several trophies and ribbons. This gave me enough confidence to consider continuing in other competitive events.

A few months later in February, 1955, my friends told me about SCCA road races in Iowa City. Thinking nothing of the over four-hour round-trip drive from Minneapolis, I remember thinking, "This sounds like fun," so with a friend, we drove down to Iowa City. When we pulled into the parking area at the event, I was amazed to see the variety of sports cars that arrived for the race. I'd never seen so many foreign race cars including Porsches, Triumphs, Maseratis, and Jaguars. I watched the races and walked around the paddock admiring the race cars, most of which I was not familiar with. I had entered the race, but for some reason decided not to subject myself or my MG to the competition. I came away impressed by the cars, the racing, the excitement of the competition, and the atmosphere. I thought to myself, "This looks like fun and something I could do; I'll have to try it again in the near future."

Racer and friend, Don Skogmo (R)

40 · *Press On... Regardless!*

Two well-known lady racers I would meet, Denise McCluggage (L) and Ruth Levy. Levy and I were the authors of the first newsletter for the Land O' Lakes SCCA Region called the Tonneau, 'it covers everything'

Bundled up ready for ice racing on Lake Phalen, on the left is my lifelong friend Paul Holtan

My awards from ice racing with the Land O' Lakes sports car club events

I took these photos at the Iowa City sports car races. I was amazed at the number and variety of different race cars present including the Maserati (above), OSCA and a Lancia (below) – exotic cars I had never seen before

ROTC

As if academics, summer camp, cars, and sports weren't enough, I joined the Air Force ROTC, in my junior year at U of M and rapidly moved up in rank. Perhaps my decision to join was influenced by the not-too-distant memory of World War II and the Korean War. In addition, my cousin was a World War II fighter pilot ace who was shot down in Europe and captured. He escaped, but was shot down again and recaptured, this time linking up with the local partisans and making his way back to the allied lines. After the war, he moved into jets with the rank of Lt. Colonel in the Air Force with 5000 hours in single engine fighters. He also served time as the "Slot Man" while flying with the U.S. Air Force Aerobatic Team, the Thunderbirds. At the time war broke out in Vietnam, he was the highest-ranking Air Force Officer and Commander in that area, helping to train new pilots.

After joining the ROTC, I became the most gung-ho cadet you ever met in your life. I did everything. I was invited to join the Arnold Air Society (Honorary Air Force Fraternity) and became its commander; I founded the first Angels Wing in the U.S. which opened the door for women to join the society; I started "The Tail Spinner," the Air Force newspaper. I moved up to the rank of cadet major in my junior year which was the first time that had ever happened.

ROTC in college then into the Air Force after graduation

Chapter 3 – Sports Cars & ROTC • **43**

Even though I had visions of becoming a pilot, there was a complication – I was color blind. An Air Force policy about this condition prevented me from obtaining a commission in the regular Air Force, so flying was out. After returning from a near perfect Air Force summer camp in Waco, Texas, I was told I would be receiving a commission in the Air National Guard (not the Air Force!!!). I was furious when I heard this and made this fact known...it almost got me tossed out of the corps. I refused to hold meetings of the Arnold Society, would not publish the Tail Spinner, and, since being in the ROTC meant I was effectively on active duty (two years in college, two years when out), I was notified I would be court martialed. The court voted to have me tossed out of the service but did not have the authority.

COLONEL KERMIT D. STEVENS

Instead, it sent its recommendation to Colonel Kermit D. Stevens who was head of the University of Minnesota's Aeronautics and Tactics Program and my ROTC Commander. Fortunately, I had a good relationship with Col. Stevens since he loved my playing Boogie Woogie on the piano. Whenever we had a party, meeting, or invited the staff, he wanted me to play the piano for him and we developed that kind of rapport. So when I met with Col. Stevens, he said, "Cole, what am I going to do with you? Did you know you were being considered for Cadet Colonel?" He allowed me to stay in the program, and much to the amazement of my friends in the corps, particularly those in the Arnold Air Society, I continued heading up the group through my senior year even though I no longer had a rank.

Press On... Regardless!

– CHAPTER FOUR –
GO WEST YOUNG MAN

Upon graduating from college in 1955, I received my Second Lieutenant commission in the Air Force (after they reversed the policy against color blindness) and was assigned to the Recruiting Service for the Air Force as the Public Information Officer (PIO) stationed in, of all places, San Francisco. I remember receiving and reading the assignment papers and couldn't believe my good luck. All my buddies were assigned to radar stations in Canada or North Dakota and here I get a plum job in San Francisco! Wanna bet my ROTC commanding officer, Col. Stevens, must have had something to do with my receiving this assignment?

I packed my bags, bid farewell to my parents, sold my trusty MG, and drove out to San Francisco with some buddies to my new life and job. Getting settled and making new friends came about quickly. I was fortunate to find a place to stay renting a room in Kent Diehl's house. His house was on Wolfback Ridge in Sausalito with a very Bohemian decor inside and offered spectacular views of the Bay Area.

Diehl was the Boating Editor for the San Francisco Chronicle and also a writer, which leads to a story. One day I received a telephone call from Kent asking me to join him for a visit to an ex-lighthouse and bring my camera. He was working on a story for the San Francisco Chronicle newspaper about the lighthouses around the San Francisco area.

Our destination was the old lighthouse on One Mile Rock, which is off the coastline and outside the Golden Gate Bridge. The only way to get to the lighthouse back then was by boat, in this case a Coast Guard Cutter. The lighthouse had a ramp extending from it to allow access to the building (see photo on previous page).

The cutter had a large opening on the ship's bow which allowed a person to exit the boat onto the lighthouse ramp. The trick was to synchronize the movement of the boat with the waves and at just the right moment, make the leap from the boat to the ramp and when reboarding the boat, do the reverse.

Fortunately, I was able to make my exit from the cutter just right and make it onto the ramp, which Kent was able to do as well. We finished our inspection and photo shoot, then were successful leaving the ramp and getting back on board the cutter...one such experience was enough for me!!

NEW WHEELS

Of course, I was in need of transportation for my new job, so one of my first stops was to Don Wilheim's Continental Cars on Van Ness Avenue in the city. Sitting on the showroom floor was a nearly new Triumph TR2 in British Racing Green with red leather interior, wire wheels with narrow white wall tires...what a beauty. It just so happened the dealer's banker was visiting that day, and I was introduced to him. During our conversation, I expressed my enthusiasm for the TR2, so the banker invited me to his office at the bank to talk further about the car. As manager of several Bank of America branches in San Francisco, his office was very lavish with a large desk, wood paneling, and brass fittings on the walls. By the time we finished the conversation, I had a loan for the car with insurance. Perhaps the fact I was in my Air Force uniform had something to do with it. I was a Lieutenant in the Air Force, stationed in San Francisco, and now owner of a nearly new TR2. Could life get any better?

NETWORKING

Another stroke of good luck was meeting Josh Hogue while visiting Kjell Qvale's British Motor Cars showroom in San Francisco. Hogue was the motor sports writer for the San Francisco Chronicle newspaper and a valuable contact to make. After learning I was a new arrival in town and of my past sports car activities in Minnesota, Hogue invited me to join him for lunch with a group of other enthusiasts at Andy Young's Kuo Wah Cafe in Chinatown. Turns out the group was known as "The Lower Grant Avenue Improvement Society" and met for lunch on a regular basis to talk sports cars and related activities. These members all owned sports cars and

Chapter 4 — Go West Young Man

were active in local events including road racing. This was another stroke of good luck to have made acquaintances with a key group of enthusiasts so soon after my arrival in town. In just a few short months, I had moved to San Francisco, found an apartment, bought a nearly new sports car, and now was involved with a sports car club. Life was definitely on a fast track.

I remember a visit to Qvale's used car showroom one day where I saw a nice Buick convertible on the showroom floor. Josh Hogue happened to be there as well standing at the back of the car. Suddenly the car started to shake, the window glass was moving in and out, I couldn't believe what was happening! In reality, I was experiencing my first earthquake... welcome to San Francisco!

BIG EVENTS

As the Public Information Officer for the Northern California office of the Air Force, I was in charge of all publicity for the Recruiting Service. My right-hand man was a Master Sergeant, Carl. W. Toole, a real Irish character who took me under his wing and helped me a lot. In my position, I made regular contact with the key people in all forms of media including the one local TV station, KPIX. The first really big job was to coordinate a nationally televised half-time show at Kezar Stadium in San Francisco, home of the San Francisco 49ers football team. The agenda started with the General from nearby Hamilton Field Air Force Base leading the swearing-in ceremony of new recruits along with the Air Force marching band and drill squad. It was a big deal, and we ran over our allotted TV time by 15 minutes which really annoyed the TV folks, but the Air Force officials enjoyed the extra exposure, much to my credit.

My second large event was to organize and coordinate the International Air Force Association Convention at the Fairmont Hotel. Master Sergeant Toole, or "Mr. Shenanigans" as I called him, was a former waist gunner on a B-17 in World War II. He and I moved our office to the hotel for a month to prepare for this event. The attendees came from all over the world; we saw more brass than you could imagine. It was a big, big event, but it went off perfectly and we had the time of our lives.

A PIANO INTERLUDE

After work one day, I decided to drop in at Barnaby Conrad's El Matador on Broadway in San Francisco. It was a popular nightclub spot with good, live music supplied by piano player Johnny Cooper and a really outstanding bass player, Vernon Alley, who would eventually become very well known in the music world. Johnny, who owned an Austin Healey, and I met at one of the local sports car functions, and he invited me to drop in and see him at the El Matador. Since he knew I was a piano player, he asked me to sit in for him when it was his break time. So, I'd sit in and play the piano and when Alley heard me playing, he would begin to play along, and we'd have a great time. Those visits to the El Matador were a very special way to spend an evening.

WEST COAST COMPETITION

I heard about an upcoming event in Willits, California, a small town about three hours north of San Francisco. The event was a gymkhana which I was basically familiar with from my Minnesota experience. It is sort of a sports car Olympics based on driver skill more than speed. There were a large number of sports cars present and after watching some of the action, I got up the nerve to enter the event about five minutes before the entries closed. I paid my two dollars and showed them my Land O'Lakes SCCA Membership card and was ready to go. I ended up tied for the top time of the day and realized I could compete with the west coast drivers whom I had thought were above my level.

With one event under my belt and full of enthusiasm and a positive attitude, I was ready for a real road race. Even as a member of the Land O'Lakes SCCA Region from Minnesota, I still had to earn a San Francisco Region racing license, which I did. I signed up for the races at Buchanan Field, the public airport in Concord, a small town across the bay from San Francisco. I brought along my cousin's helmet to wear in the race. (Remember, he was an ex-fighter pilot ace and an Air Force Lt. Colonel.) I was proud to wear his helmet, but in retrospect, it looked like it was made of papier-mâché and likely offered very little protection.

In my Triumph TR2 ready to go onto the track
Buchanan Field first-place trophy

I was entered in and won the all-Triumph Class race, my first road race victory but not my last by a long shot. As a race winner, I was invited to race in the Modified Class, but I almost didn't make this race since my tires were virtually worn out. One of my friends from the Triangle Sports Car Club (Race, Show, Rally) I cofounded had an Austin Healey, so I borrowed his tires and wheels in order to compete in the race. I ran well up in the field and, combined with my first class victory, it was a successful weekend. That first win was very significant for me and in fact I still have the trophy I was presented on my desk at my shop (see photo opposite page).

A VERY AUSPICIOUS MEETING

At these races, I met three people who would play a role in my future racing career. The first two were husband and wife team Jim and Marion Lowe, both seasoned road racers, very competitive drivers, and very involved with the San Francisco Region of the SCCA. The third was Rusty Hyde, the Triumph Sub-Distributor for Northern California. Hyde had watched me race at Buchanan Field and felt he might have discovered a driver with good potential. He walked over and introduced himself to me and offered to help further my racing aspirations. Rusty asked if I would be interested in racing a modified TR2 along with my own Production Class TR2. I couldn't say yes fast enough. This was not only the beginning of a great and productive friendship, but also my long association with Triumph race cars and British cars in general.

Embroidered SCCA patch

Chapter 4 – Go West Young Man • 53

KJELL QVALE

Kjell Qvale – (Shell Kah-VAH-lee) – I've always wanted to put that in print! I first met Kjell in 1955 shortly after I arrived in SF for my Air Force assignment at 30 Van Ness Avenue. I was 22 years old and had competed successfully on the ice in my MG TD on Lake Phalen at the Saint Paul Winter Carnival in Minnesota. Therefore, I felt I had the "creds" to walk into his dealership on Van Ness Avenue and introduce myself.

Kjell was part of the Lower Grant Avenue Improvement Society with Josh Hogue, and we began a friendship that lasted until his passing in 2013. Kjell was the owner of British Motor Car Distributors, Inc., which he founded in 1948 in San Bruno, California. Oddly enough, in 1963 I founded Bob Cole Motor Imports in... San Bruno. In my role as PIO for the Air Force, I naturally was in constant contact with what then made up the mass media – newspapers, radio, magazines and the one fledgling TV Station, KPIX Channel 5.

In 1956, I was appointed Assistant Regional Executive of the SF Region SCCA in charge of press and publicity. It was after the death of Ernie McAfee while racing in the forest at Pebble Beach (I raced there that weekend in my TR3) and the cessation of racing on those streets, that the Sports Car Racing Association of the Monterey Peninsula (SCRAMP) was formed and, in collaboration with the SCCA, efforts took shape to move the races to a new venue called Laguna Seca.

Kjell was a big part of that endeavor, and I was called upon to be the messenger to the public. However, in early 1957, I was discharged from the Air Force (as a 24-year-old Captain) and decided (for reasons not clear to me now) to return to the University of Minnesota to pursue a Master's degree. Kjell was not pleased to learn of this and, in his indomitable and some would say obdurate manner, phoned me and rather insisted I return because of Laguna Seca. He proffered me a job at $600 a month as well as a few perks and after a discussion with my father, I decided to return to San Francisco! So, it can be said that Kjell Qvale is responsible for, or demanding, my return, and I have never once regretted having done so. As it turned out, we were successful in opening Laguna Seca later that year with a huge, opening day crowd and the rest they say is history. Thank you, Kjell!

On a sidenote involving Kjell, I had heard from a few of his friends that he was not known to laugh. As a result, I took it upon myself to inject some humor in my conversations with him to provoke a smile or laugh and eventually I succeeded on several occasions. When I would meet Kjell at business functions after becoming a car dealer, he would greet me with a hug. When my friend Bob Devlin saw such a greeting, he told me he had never seen Kjell hug anyone else. Guess I made a favorable impression on him.

At one of the early San Francisco Import Car Shows which Kjell started and owned, he asked me to be on the Board of Directors. He also asked me to introduce his two young sons to visiting Formula One driver Graham Hill at the event. I was honored he asked me to do so and pleased to meet such a celebrity as well. Kjell was a unique and very successful businessman whom I was fortunate to meet and develop a long-standing friendship with.

Kjell Qvale had a big influence on my early career

The Fire Boid on display, Oakland Roadster Show, me on the far right

Me on the far left

Press On... Regardless!

– CHAPTER FIVE –
CHANGE OF DIRECTION

AN UNUSUAL ASSIGNMENT

Early in 1956, I received a message from the U.S. Air Force Strategic Air Command (SAC) HQ in Omaha, Nebraska. SAC was headed by General Curtis LeMay who had his PIO, bird Colonel Reed Tilley, search the Air Force ranks for someone familiar with race cars. Somehow Tilley found me and sent the message that General LeMay wanted me back in Omaha to advise how the Air Force could use a special race car in recruiting. LeMay had authorized the use of U.S. Air Force bases for sports car racing and the Air Force had acquired a former Indianapolis race car and married it to a gas turbine engine to produce a most unique tool for use in recruiting young people to join the Air Force. The objective was to show the race car at events around the country to enlighten young men about high-tech career opportunities in the Air Force.

I remained in Omaha for one month as the car was completed, and I helped develop a program for its use in recruiting. Colonel Tilley, who was a great guy, wanted me to stay in Omaha and work with him. He said, "You know Bob, it would only take one call from General LeMay, and you would be here." I pondered his offer of staying in Omaha and essentially starting a new life or returning to my friends, racing, and my job in San Francisco. Plus, the climate and environment were better in San Francisco, so I bid Omaha adieu and returned to my post in San Francisco.

The car, now called "Fire Boid," was sent to Indianapolis Speedway for testing and then used for exhibition laps at the 1955 Indianapolis 500 race. It never did race but was sent out on a nationwide tour for Air Force recruiting. One year later, the car and I were reunited at the Oakland Roadster Show where it attracted a good number of attendees to the Air Force recruiting display.

MAJOR THACKER S. SCALES

Major Scales was my commanding officer in the Air Force Recruiting office in San Francisco. He made sure I understood he did not appreciate my being fresh out of college and already a commissioned officer, something he had to work long and hard for. He came up through the ranks and received a battlefield commission and had a dim view of young, fresh-faced officers. As a result, we did not have the "warmest" of relationships. However, there were several situations that arose during my short tour of duty with the Air Force in San Francisco that kept the Major from being a problem.

The first two situations have been described in the previous chapter (see Big Events, pg. 50) – the events at Kezar Stadium and the International Air Force Convention, both in San Francisco. Each event gave me the opportunity to meet with several high ranking officers attending the event. Having these contacts would be an asset if I needed their help in the future and of course Major Scales was aware of these contacts.

The third situation came as a surprise to me when Scales called me into his office one day and handed me a telegram from my cousin, Lt. Colonel "Tink" Cole, who was the commander of FLYTAF (Flight Training Air Force) for the Air Force. Tink was flying a two-seat, F80/T33 Shooting Star jet fighter and would be picking me up the next Saturday morning at Alameda Naval Air Station. When I met Tink, he told me we were going to fly back to Minnesota to have dinner with my family and spend the night. The next day we would fly down to Lackland AFB in Texas before returning to San Francisco. While at Lackland, Tink thought I should become a pilot but even though he tried his hardest to see about getting me into the program, it just wasn't feasible due to my being color blind. So Major Scales knew I was associated with more high-ranking officers, and he began to wonder just who was this Lt. Bob Cole?

Cousin Tink – WWII fighter ace and career Air Force officer

58 • *Press On... Regardless!*

Of course, having General Curtis LeMay request I come to SAC HQ in Omaha, Nebraska, must have really put Major Scales into a state. He certainly made it known upon my return after a month away he didn't appreciate my being gone so long, but he couldn't think of making it an issue.

The last situation involved a family friend from Minnesota, Norma Lundeen, who had been married to our state Senator Ernest Lundeen. They were friends of our family when I was growing up. After her husband died in a plane crash, she eventually remarried another Senator, Rufus C. Hollman of Oregon. I remember her as an ebullient, outgoing larger-than-life woman.

Sitting at my desk in the Air Force Recruiting office one day, I heard a woman in a loud voice say, "Bobbie!" When I turned around, Norma gave me a big hug and introduced me to her husband, the Senator. Well, this was the topper for Major Scales and solidified my position as a young man with high-level military and government contacts. I'm sure he was happy to see me receive my discharge from the Air Force in early 1957.

1956 – A FULL RACING SCHEDULE

Prior to the racing season, Rusty Hyde took a TR2 to Bill Breeze's Sports Car Center in Sausalito to have the car modified and prepared for racing. Since I had been more or less "hired" by Hyde as an amateur driver, I helped strip the car to the frame, which was then lightened, the track widened, the engine modified, larger carburetors fitted, and four-wheel Dunlop disc brakes from a Jaguar D-type installed, all of which would give us a big advantage over other drum brake cars.

I also had that different helmet to wear – my cousin Tink's Air Force pilot helmet was an improvement over the early "brain bucket" we all wore in those early days. Tink's helmet at least covered the whole head but was made of pretty flimsy material, so it didn't offer a great deal more as far as safety was concerned.

Looking back, it is amazing that in less than six months after arriving in San Francisco, I made several key contacts, added a sponsor, bought a new TR3, had available a TR2 to race, and earned my first race trophy. It seems the Air Force assignment to San Francisco was working out rather well.

Santa Rosa Airport races and me in #88

Along with a couple of my sports car friends, we started "The Triangle Sports Car Club" with the slogan, "we cover all the angles – shows, racing and rallies." We had triangle shaped badges made up for the members but mine has disappeared over time.

The Hyde/Cole Partnership decided to contest a full season in 1956 racing both my TR3 and Hyde's modified TR2 in production and modified classes respectively. This was an ambitious schedule considering most of the tracks and drivers would be new to me and I would be racing two essentially untested cars. Nonetheless, we pressed on with races scheduled at Stockton, Palm Springs, Santa Barbara, Santa Rosa, Pebble Beach, Buchanan Field, Arcata, and Sacramento.

I knew the level of competition in the Modified Class was going to be tough and that was validated at Palm Springs when I lined up last on the grid behind the top West Coast drivers of the day including Carroll Shelby, Dan Gurney, Bob Oker, Max Balchowski, Phil Hill, John von Neumann, and Jack McAfee. I had a great race with Oker, a well-known, talented driver from Southern California. We were pretty evenly matched, since both of us were in Triumphs... but I had one advantage – my car had disc brakes versus his car's drum brakes.

With the race underway, Oker passed me on the second lap which was not what I had in mind. As we raced down the straightaway, I was on the outside with Oker running alongside to

The way we traveled to races in the Rusty Hyde provided tow rig

my right. Since his car was a left-hand drive version, his exhaust was in front of the left side wheel where I could plainly hear it. As we headed towards an upcoming turn, I thought I could out-brake him since I had disc brakes. Listening to his exhaust sound, I could tell when he let off the gas to brake so I waited for that moment, then I hit the brakes and succeeded in out braking him and made the pass. Unfortunately, my modified TR2 suffered a broken rocker arm, and I was forced out of the race. Oker continued for a few more laps until his car also suffered a mechanical failure. It was a good race while it lasted!

At the end of the year, we did pretty well, with podium finishes and trophies to take home. Our two Triumphs were continually refined throughout the year as were my driving skills. Plus, I learned each car's nuances and the characteristics of each race venue.

These are the two cars I raced in 1956, a production model and a modified car. The latter is the one I raced against Bob Oker

Chapter 5 – Change Of Direction • 61

YEAR OF CHANGES

1957 was a year of change for me with an interesting twist mid-year that reshaped my career path. The year started out normally enough with my job in the Air Force and preparing the race cars for the upcoming racing season. I raced the first two events of the new season at Stockton followed by Cotati where I also had new responsibilities as a co-founder of the Rules Enforcement Committee. Myself and the other co-founder, Bob Winkelmann, decided to create several new rules governing technical inspection at each race necessitated by more drivers "deviating" from the rule book. To add credibility to tech inspection, our new rules included weighing each car and testing fuel along with other changes to help make the racing fair for everyone. We found that the middle of the pack did most of the cheating. The San Francisco Region Technical Inspection Rules were eventually adopted by the SCCA National Office and utilized throughout the country.

In early 1957, my commitment to the Air Force was completed, so I was discharged with the rank of Captain and became a civilian once again. Even though I enjoyed San Francisco, my many friends, and sports car racing, I decided to return to Minnesota and enroll in college to pursue a Master's degree in Psychology. I packed up my TR3 and headed to Minnesota where I enrolled at the University of Minnesota. However, this path to higher education did not last long.

Approximately one month later, I received that unexpected phone call from Kjell Qvale, who was also deeply involved with the San Francisco Region (SFR) of the SCCA. Qvale was one of the SFR members who was working on a plan to develop a new purpose-

Cotati in May, I had a good race with the Jag

built racetrack in the Monterey area after the Pebble Beach races were canceled. Qvale was not aware I had left San Francisco, thus the phone call. Qvale said, "We need you back here right now. You know about the Laguna Seca proposal and with all your media contacts, you are the only guy that can help us get the word out. You know all the press people; we need you for Laguna Seca."

He offered me a job, company car, expenses, and position as PR and Advertising Manager for his company. I would work for BMCD but also handle the PR and publicity for the SFR SCCA. I accepted his offer and returned to San Francisco and my new job.

LAGUNA SECA

In addition to my new job with BMCD, I was also contacted by one of my local racing friends, Jimmy Orr. I had met Orr within the first few months after arriving in San Francisco and we became friends. For 1957, Orr had been elected as the Regional Executive for the SFR and with Qvale's help, he appointed me as the Assistant Regional Executive in charge of press and publicity.

Due to my extensive contacts with motor sports reporters in radio, television, newspapers, and magazines, I slipped right into my new job. I had regularly been in contact with all forms of media supplying race results from SFR events along with the latest club and racing news. With the closing of the Pebble Beach race course after the 1956 race, local Monterey business and government leaders quickly sprang into action to find another road race venue to continue and grow both the sports car races and the Pebble Beach Concours.

A new organization in Monterey, the Sport Car Racing at Monterey Peninsula (SCRAMP), was tasked with finding a new venue and funding the construction of a new racetrack. Once the Laguna Seca site at Fort Ord had been selected and approved, I became an important conduit for information presented to the public as the project developed. With the SFR essentially hired to organize and run the races, I attended both SFR and SCRAMP meetings to chronicle the groups' progress and report to the media.

I remember one trip down to Monterey to look at the new track site – a group of us drove from the Bay Area, arriving early

Jim Lowe's San Francisco Region SCCA "company vehicle" I borrowed

in the morning. The fog was thick so we had our headlights on, but we could barely see the road and wondered where the site was. Suddenly the fog broke and there was this natural earthen "bowl" with a dry lake in the middle – Laguna Seca. Surveying the area, it was easy to see most of the proposed track since there weren't a lot of trees. All the construction crew really had to do to create the racetrack was pave the dirt roads that were already there.

During another group visit to the track while construction was in progress, I was part of a discussion about the direction the race cars would circulate around the track. Since most European and American racetracks ran in a clockwise direction, I had already ordered my new race car, a right-hand drive TR3, which would give me a bit of an advantage on a course with mostly right-hand turns. However, after seeing the Corkscrew take shape, I realized it would be no advantage since I knew we couldn't run the course clockwise which meant going up the Corkscrew then making a blind, 90-degree right-hand turn. In the end, the powers that be decided to run the course in the counter-clockwise direction and it has remained the same to this day. There are several stories about who came up with the name for the series of turns now known around the world as "The Corkscrew." However, no one really knows who was the first to come up with the name, but it became the signature turn at Laguna Seca which is still the case today.

Once the opening day for the new road course was established, it was my responsibility to get the word out through all my media contacts and create the cover for the event program. For the program cover photo, a site was chosen with an ocean view as a backdrop with three Jaguar cars positioned in the foreground. I selected two street models and one race car (which I am seated in) to represent the sports car races and the Concours d'Elegance. The

The original Laguna Seca track configuration with a very fast turn 2, flat out only for the brave

Chapter 5 – Change Of Direction • 65

Midway through the Corkscrew, I am leading John Luce, Wm. Kinchelow, Lew Spencer, Peter Culken, and Dr. George Snively.

races were an outstanding success on the new Laguna Seca track and a new era had arrived for racing in Northern California. Of course, the Pebble Beach Concours continued and has grown to become – arguably – the number one event of its kind in the world. Additionally, I was part of the original founders of Sears Point International Raceway.

SPORTS CAR MAGAZINE NATIONAL AWARD

During my tenure as the Head of Public Relations for the San Francisco Region of the SCCA, I wrote several articles for the SCCA national magazine Sports Car. One of the articles which appeared in the January/February 1958 issue titled "Gilding the Retired Lily... 8th Pebble Beach" was a race report about the inaugural race at the new Laguna Seca Raceway which opened on November 7, 1957. This article won the magazine's national award for best article of the year.

Jan/Feb 1958 issue of Sports Car magazine

65,000 spectators witness the first running of the new Laguna Seca course at Ft. Ord, California. The 30 foot wide ribbon, (with 30 foot shoulders), weaves its winding way around nine turns up and downhill, and provides what is probably one of the most interesting panorama of sports car racing in this country.

SAN FRANCISCO REGION —
Gilding a Retired Lily...8th Pebble Beach
by BOB COLE
with STAN & MIDGE LEWIS

PEBBLE BEACH, an appelation that mantles a true sense of fame, dignity, respect and prestige; that connotes a message of international renown to sports car enthusiasts in many far-off corners, realized this year it's octennial anniversary, November 9-10, at an unfamiliar place called Laguna Seca. Located on leased government land, and physically positioned within a few miles of the old Del Monte Forest course, the new 1.6 mile circuit at Laguna Seca provided the necessaries to perpetuate a sports car racing tradition. True, the title "Pebble Beach" is somewhat of a misnomer to those who have not experienced what is truly "Pebble's," and therefore have not the reasons for carrying on the name. The weekend's attendant activities are far too numerous to describe in these notes; however, suffice it to say that it was strongly felt, since this was the second oldest consecutive road race in this country, (Watkins Glen heading the list), coupled with the very cogent fact that the equally famous Concours D'Elegance would again be held at Del Monte Lodge, the name of Pebble Beach would immediately serve to identify the continuance of the West Coast's Blue Ribbon Classic of sports car racing. Sponsorship was provided through the very capable and untiring efforts of SCRAMP, (the initialized condensation of the Sports Car Racing Association of the Monterey Peninsula). SCRAMP is the liaison body for the Monterey Chamber of Commerce that performed so very well the necessary functions vital to the projected rebirth of the famed sports car weekend at Pebble Beach. It is mainly through and because of their efforts that the new course was realized.

It is truly unpredictable what extent of success this mammoth speculation will materialize into. 65,000 spectators sojourned from points South, North and East to experience with us the magnificent display of circumstance these races always provide. They were wonderous at the site before them; fully 60-70% of the course could be seen from many of the excellent vantage points!

The event was surfeited with all the pageantry and spectacle that suggests Pebble Beach. It was also burdened with elements that sponsor fond remembrances of past Pebble's, and more realistically, elements that nourish the senses to maintain a continued vitalization and a never ending public interest in the activities at Laguna Seca that "gild the retired lily" of Pebble Beach. Portrayed below are the expressions registered in vivid capture by one of the 65,000, after his attendance at this magnificent sports car race. The profundities of his remarks are surprisingly accurate and yet result from a first visit to a sports car race!

*"Yesterday was of another century. Where there was beauty and elegance, today there is only a leaden sky, the desert hills and the crooked oval of the black track that wanders a double mile.

"Where there was quiet, today there is a snarling

*George Baker, S. F. Argonaut

– CHAPTER FIVE –
PHOTO GALLERY

In #111 next to James Lowe, Arcata 1956

Talking with Bill Breeze (L) and Joe Richards prior to Santa Rosa race in 1956

Pebble Beach- 1956, wearing my cousin's Air Force helmet

Publicity photo for Buchanan Field 1956

Wolfback Ridge in Sausalito with San Francisco in the background, circa 1956

On the grid at Santa Barbara Airport 1955

I drove this right-hand drive Triumph and a left-hand drive model for Rusty Hyde in the same season

The always fun Cobb Mountain Hill Climb – 1956

Preparing the Triumph at Palm Springs races in 1956

Lined up for tech inspection at Pebble Beach in 1956

Chapter 5 – Change Of Direction • **69**

The above are the first pages of four articles I wrote for the SCCA national magazine Sports Car in 1957 and 1958

Above: When I stopped SCCA racing and in recognition of my racing success and contribution to the Region, I was awarded this Honorary Permanent Official Pit Pass to all San Francisco Region races

Below: Lapel pin

On the way to 5th overall and 1st in class at Cotati Enduro

I finished 5th in class in a stock MGA at the first races at Laguna Seca. This same photo was used for the cover of the next race program

Press On... Regardless!

– CHAPTER SIX –

RACING & NEW OPPORTUNITIES

BACK TO THE RACETRACK

While I shuffled between the full-time job at BMCD as head of advertising and PR, plus similar duties with the SFR, I did not have much time for racing in the 1957 season. I was able to squeeze in a few races including 3rd in class at Cotati in my TR3 in May then a class victory co-driving Jim Lowe's Lotus 11 at the Cotati 6-hour enduro in August. The Lotus was maintained and race prepared at Bill Breeze's Sports Car Center in Sausalito. Prior the event, Lowe asked me to pick up the car at Breeze's shop and take it for some "shake down" runs on the back roads of Marin County. So off I went, zipping along the two-lane roads in this street legal race car past all the watching cows as I was having a great time, all the way to Bodega Bay and back. Can you imagine being able to do this today? Not a chance!

After all the work on the Laguna Seca Project, it was gratifying to not only see the track finished but also be an entrant in the inaugural race weekend. I did not have a race car, but could not miss this opportunity to be part of local racing history. I decided to enter my virtually bone stock MGA Coupe "BMCD company car," white sidewalls and all. I surprised even myself by finishing 5th in class.

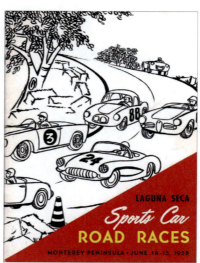

Sample of the many dash plaques I received when entering a race. My first ever race plaque in Minnesota, upper left

After a relatively light racing schedule in 1957, and with Laguna Seca Raceway firmly in operation, I felt it was time for another change in my career. My friend Rusty Hyde offered me a job as salesman at Triumph Inc., so I left BMCD. I resumed a full racing schedule which extended over the next three years in my Triumph TR3. 1958 was a breakthrough year for me with a number of first place finishes in class which some motor sports writers (including Gus Vignolle of MotoRacing) said, "...firmly established Cole as one of the drivers to beat on the West Coast."

DON SHERWOOD'S "RAID"

I had an unusual and entertaining experience in 1958 when fellow SCCA member and friend, Gene Babow, and I heard about local radio talk show host Don Sherwood's plan to conduct "The Raid on Stockton." Sherwood had a very popular radio show on station KSFO with a huge listening audience attracted by his entertaining show and colorful character. Sherwood and his traffic reporter sidekick, Hap Harper, concocted a scheme for the "armed invasion and liberation of Stockton." The idea took hold, and all sorts of people became involved as Sherwood and Harper mobilized their "invasion army."

TR4 we named "Greenie." Curley Welch (L) works on my car between races

Another class victory in the TR4, this time at the Reno-Stead Airport in my favorite race car

To assist in this effort, Babow and I felt getting involved would provide publicity for the SCCA, so we created a proclamation which we read to Sherwood at the KSFO studios, live on the air. We offered to organize the ground mobile forces to assist in the invasion which he gladly accepted. The event actually took place during the summer of 1958 with the invading army of cars, planes, boats, and even a tank "capturing" Stockton's City Hall. It was one of the greatest stunts in San Francisco radio history. Hap Harper wrote a book about Don Sherwood and devoted a section of it to the "invasion" story.

A CHANGE OF DEALERSHIPS

I decided to leave Triumph Inc. in 1959 to become the sales manager for Don Hampton's Imported Cars dealership in Palo Alto, and continued racing in a Hampton-sponsored Triumph. Without thinking much of it, my business career path was beginning to turn in a different direction. I was now in my late 20s and had already accomplished quite a bit — college graduate,

Pacific GP Trophy 1962 which resides in The Candy Store

Chapter 6 – Racing & New Opportunities • 75

a stint in the Air Force, successful racer, head of PR and marketing for a major car distributor, Assistant Regional Executive for the SFR, and now sales manager for a car dealership.

In 1962, Triumph introduced the next progression in its sports car lineup, the TR4, which would become its best-selling sports model to date. It's as if the car was made with me in mind since my racing success moved up a notch. I thoroughly dominated my class in 1962 and 1963, winning the majority of the races and finishing no lower than third place during those two years. The results included the highly competitive 1962 Pacific Grand Prix at Laguna Seca where I won the production class overall.

THE SEBRING 12 HOURS

My success while racing Triumphs, and especially the TR4, enhanced my reputation as one of the top drivers on the west coast and in the country. As a result, the Triumph Factory invited me to be a part of its three-car team managed by Kas Kastner for the 1963 Sebring 12 Hours race. Hand-picked Triumph drivers from around the country were now teamed together for the grueling endurance race with drivers assigned to each race car. I was paired with Charlie Gates and Ed Diehl for the race, sharing one of the factory TR4s with hardtops.

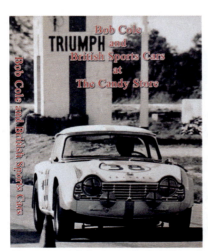

My car at Sebring passes the Triumph Tower

The poster for the Sebring 12 Hours, a race that was very exciting

Our Triumph team cars shown in an ad from Sebring 12 Hours race

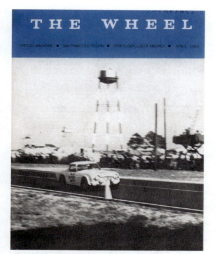

On the cover of the SF Region Magazine, from Sebring

The race initially went well, however, after several hours, Gates was driving and as he came around the last turn before the long straight, a Cobra driver was fast approaching from behind. He couldn't brake soon enough and hit the back of the TR4, shoving the exhaust system forward, which put a 90-degree upward bend in the manifold. The resultant exhaust gases burned a hole in the exhaust pipe which ignited the fiber mat covering the transmission tunnel inside the car with smoke and flame. During the night as I would downshift coming into the hairpin turn, the pit crew said they could see the inside of the car's cockpit light up when the fire would reignite.

After I took over for Gates, I smelled the fumes from the fire and returned to the pits. In the meantime, the crew had collected a number of ketchup and mustard plastic bottles, emptied them and refilled them with water. When I arrived in the pits, they poured water on the fire and put the bottles behind the seat and in the door pockets. As the fire reappeared, I'd squirt some water from the bottles onto the fire while continuing to race. We were successful in keeping the car going and finished the race in a very credible 24th overall and 2nd in class. One well-known driver from the East Coast, Bob Tullius, and I met and would become longtime

Chapter 6 – Racing & New Opportunities • 77

friends. This was an exciting week at Sebring, and it remains one of my fondest racing memories.

The pits at Sebring were run by Road & Track Magazine who did all the lap timing for us. The adjacent pit to ours was the Ferrari Team with drivers Pedro Rodriquez and Graham Hill in a front engine 4.0 Liter Ferrari. You can imagine the scene in their pits with a mixed crew of Italian and Mexican mechanics trying to work together; it was very entertaining.

Partway through the race, the Rodriquez/Hill Ferrari lost its headlights so as it approached a turn, it would close up on other cars to use its headlights. Once through the turn, the Ferrari would pull out and blast past the slower car. The speed differential was quite something, so you had to pay attention and stay to the right side of the track. The race marshalls said they could see the Ferrari's running lights, so the car was not black flagged.

After the race, Charlie Gates and I went back to our motel. As we entered the room, I said to Charlie, "That air conditioning unit is sure loud," to which he replied, "Bob, it isn't on, it's your ears that are bothering you!" He was right, I was almost deaf from all the noise in the race car during those hours on the track. It took me a couple of days to regain my normal hearing.

SPECIAL PEOPLE

JIMMY ORR

Jimmy Orr was the real estate broker extraordinaire for the upscale community of Kent Woodlands in Marin County, California. He also was the originator and developer of Stinson Beach – that exclusive enclave located on a spit of land west of California and east of the Pacific Ocean near Bodega Bay in Marin County. I recall watching the Forty Niners on that still strange invention called television at his home there!

As I was then still the Public Information Officer (PIO) for the Air Force, I had daily contact with the media and could also promote the coming event at "The Pebble Beach Road Races at Laguna Seca." We more than achieved our goal as some 37,000-47,000 enthusiasts made their way down to that remote and virtually unknown place called Fort Ord in November of 1957.

And the rest, as the proverb says, is history!

Jimmy Orr was my mentor – perhaps a father figure – and inculcated in me a sense of self worth, positivism, and courage that has served me well for all these decades. I remember him with great admiration and profound appreciation for his belief in me. We remained friends for a long time.

He was instrumental in my joining the St. Francis Yacht Club in 1972 and visited me at The Candy Store in the mid-1980s. Thank you, Jimmy.

JOE RICHARDS

Joe was the Northern California rep for Triumph Motor Cars in the 1950s and 60s. He took me under his wing and had a lot to do with my becoming a dealer. He convinced me I could, and should, do it and introduced me to the right people to make that happen. He fervently followed any racing Triumphs and was heavily involved in the decision to place me on the Triumph Factory Team for the Sebring 12 Hours race. I will always thank him, posthumously of course, for being one of the first persons to believe in me and my future.

– CHAPTER SIX –
PHOTO GALLERY

On the cover of another magazine in the TR3

From the 1957 program for Laguna Seca, I was a club officer

An advertisement that appeared in the Nevada Grand Prix extolling the success of Triumph sports cars in racing

Trophy for finishing first overall at the Vaca Valley road races in 1958

Racing the TR3 at Stockton Airport in 1957

Here I lead Ed Leslie (L) and Don Wester (Ctr) at the Stockton Road Races

Chapter 6 – Racing & New Opportunities • **81**

An advertisement from a Sears Point race program announcing our appointment as the Lotus Distributor for the Western U.S.

Racing a TR4 helped to sell the same model at our dealerships. Exiting turn 9 at Laguna Seca ahead of my friend Ron Craven's Corvette, see story p. 90-91

I finished first in class in the Don Hampton sponsored/prepared TR4 at this race at Cotati Raceway in August, 1962

Press On... Regardless!

– CHAPTER SEVEN –
ON MY OWN

BECOMING A CAR DEALER

While working for Don Hampton's Imported Cars dealership as sales manager, part of my job was to stay in regular contact with my Triumph distributor friend Joe Richards. As noted at the end of Chapter 6, Richards convinced me I had the experience and background to become a car dealership owner and mentioned there was a small dealer in San Bruno (town close by San Francisco) that was failing. Suggesting this would be good opportunity for me, Richards felt I ought to consider buying it. This certainly was an intriguing thought and a good opportunity to branch out on my own, however, I would need some assistance... enter Rod Carveth.

One facet of amateur racing in the 1950s and 1960s which made the sport attractive and fun was the friendships that were developed among teammates and competitors alike. I had met Rod Carveth, a well-known SFR racer in the late 1950s, and we developed a friendship that would last for many years. Carveth owned a popular and successful sports car parts and accessory business on the San Francisco peninsula. One of his employees who worked in the parts department was John Mozart, who was the son of Gus Mozart, an acquaintance of mine and a VW and Porsche dealer. At that time John was a 17-year-old kid who would

Rod Carveth circa 1957

Chapter 7 – On My Own • 85

LOTUS PARTS

We have purchased the complete parts stock of Lotus on the West Coast.

Rod Carveth Enterprises

770 El Camino Real • San Carlos • LYtell 1-8921
Open Monday through Saturday from 8 a.m. till 6 p.m.

---

later become a commercial real estate entrepreneur and own a large collection of great classic cars and memorabilia.

Gus Mozart's partner in the VW and Porsche dealership, Emil Pardee, asked me at one point if I wanted to become the general manager of his new VW dealership in South Lake Tahoe. It was a nice offer which I appreciated, but I declined the invitation. That was the right decision considering what happened shortly thereafter which was already in the mix.

The idea of becoming a dealer had stuck with me and I recall saying to myself, "You really enjoy cars and always have, maybe you should stick with it." Then Joe Richards convinced me I could do it. I gave the idea serious consideration, but I lacked one important element – the necessary capital to buy the failing dealership myself. So, I turned to Carveth and my father for assistance. They each contributed $10,000 and I sold three of my personal cars which brought in enough money along with help from Bank of America to buy the dealership. The year was 1963, and I had become a dealership owner at the age of 30, a rather remarkable achievement in those days considering I had graduated from college less than ten years earlier.

THE BUSINESS TAKES HOLD

Bob Cole Motor Imports initially sold Triumph, Alfa Romeo, SAAB, Morgan, and Lotus (from Carveth). I also sold an occasional Ferrari ordered from Bill Harrah who was the distributor for Nevada and Northern California. I recall bringing the first Ferrari Daytona into California from Harrah. I had to have the car checked by California DMV to make sure all the lights met its standards! I sold the car to Howard Arneson, founder of the Arneson Pool Sweep Company, for $24,000 in 1965...what are they worth now?

I used my friends at Bank of America to floor the inventory and continued building relationships with additional banks which would play an important part in the coming years. Initially the dealership was staffed with only two people, myself and friend Wayne Reynolds who had multiple roles as the parts and service manager and the only mechanic. I was now on my way in a career I did not see coming just a few years earlier.

I made several business trips to the UK to further my relationship with the car manufacturers I represented. The contacts I made helped me get the jump on my competition or react quickly to an opportunity. A case in point happened with Lotus when I flew in the first Lotus Elan streetcar imported to the U.S. from the factory in the UK, which was quickly sold to a customer. On one of my trips to the UK, I attended the Earls Court Motor Show where I saw for the first time the Lotus Cortina MK1 SE. After meeting Colin Chapman (yes, THAT Colin Chapman) founder of Lotus, I purchased a special, high-performance version of the car. I bought the car with the idea I might keep it and now, five decades later, I still have the same car in my personal collection today. It is a rare model, one of only 16 made with the Sport Equipment (SE) Package. The Cortina was built in the original Lotus factory in

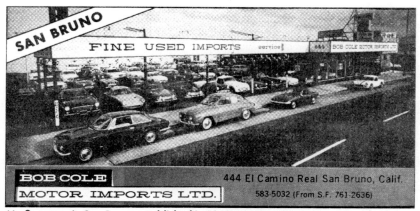

My first store in San Bruno established in 1963

Cheshunt before moving to Norwich which I visited on a few trips to England. The original key fob for the car says Cheshunt.

Having good contacts with my suppliers also brought about other opportunities. In 1963 or 1964, I received a call from Ron Richardson, Lotus International Sales Manager, who requested I visit the factory to discuss a business proposition. After arriving in the UK and meeting with Richardson and General Manager Freddie Bushell, I was asked to be part of a new company that would import certain "small vehicle motor" British cars into the U.S. including Reliant, Lotus, Jensen, Morgan, etc. Ultimately the Small Vehicle Motor Association (SVMA) plan did not pan out, but I was able to take advantage of the situation by meeting a number of the proposed car manufacturers while I was there. It was Bushell who loaned me a Lotus Cortina to drive around to visit the various companies and later he became involved in the DeLorean Motor Car legal proceedings when they went bankrupt.

Chapman died of a heart attack after returning from a Formula One meeting in Paris, flying home on a private plane. Seems that due to bad weather, the pilot did not want to land the plane at the

The Lotus Cortina – I purchased this car directly from Colin Chapman while attending the Earl's Court Car Show (Roy Dryer painting)

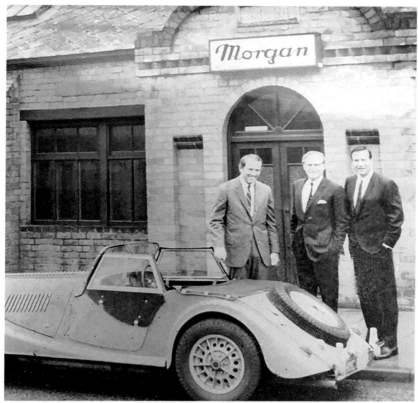
Morgan factory – Frank Gyorgy (L), Peter Morgan (M) and me (R)

Frank Gyorgy and me at our Morgan Booth at the San Francisco International Car Show in Brooks Hall, circa 1965/1966

Chapter 7 – On My Own • **89**

designated airfield, so Chapman took the controls and landed the plane. He later died at home. Upon hearing the news, Bushell went to the Lotus offices in Norwich and allegedly destroyed documents that could have compromised his and Chapman's position with regards to their involvement with DeLorean.

One of my visits was to Jensen Motors where a lunch was held for myself and the representatives from Lotus. While on a tour, I was shown a secret project, a prototype single overhead camshaft, four-cylinder engine destined for a small sports car. When I returned home, I had a meeting with Kjell Qvale to discuss the SVMA. I mentioned the engine and Qvale was quite interested. Apparently, he had been looking for such a product for the as yet released Jensen Healey where the engine found a home.

Speaking of engines, when I, along with my then partner Frank Gyorgy, visited the Morgan Motor Company, we met with Peter Morgan. While on a factory tour, I saw the first Morgan with a Buick V8 engine installed which was a secret project at that time.

RACE ON SUNDAY...

I would not be the first dealership owner to also road race, there were others in Northern California including Carveth, Sam Weiss, Ed Leslie, and Don Wester. However, unlike some of the dealership owners/racers, I was racing a production car of the type I also sold and which spectators could easily identify with. 1963 was a very successful racing season and at the end of the year, I was ranked number one in my class by the Road Racing Drivers Club for the San Francisco Region. On a humorous note, my friend Ron

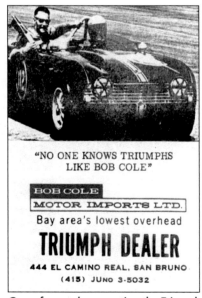

One of our ads promoting the Triumph brand and our location in San Bruno. John Carr with me

Craven (in his Corvette) and I (in my Triumph) raced in the same production race many times over two years. However, he could never beat me. So he finally bought a set of Bob Cole Motor Imports license plate frames to put on his Corvette!! My success combined with the highly popular TR4 awaiting customers in my showroom were two factors that helped to move a good number of these cars through my dealership.

Triumph awarded its top U.S. dealers with a two-week trip to England and Europe. We had red carpet treatment the whole time which included stops in New York, London, Paris, Rome, Madrid, and Monaco.

CLOSING MY RACING CAREER

In 1964 my favorite race car, the TR4, and I dominated my class races again adding further credibility to the Triumph brand name which benefited my dealership. The same year saw an expansion of the dealership staff including Dennis Harrington to head up the Service Department, mechanic Jimmy Griffin, and Frank Gyorgy as a salesman and minor partner. Jimmy maintained my Lotus Cortina and is currently tuning it up for me.

Above: Curley Welch

Right: The cover page of the special ad I placed in Autoweek to correspond with the San Francisco Import Car Show

Chapter 7 – On My Own

While 1964 would be my last full-time racing season, my business was expanding, and I needed to focus more of my time on it. In 1965 I won my last race at Laguna Seca, my favorite racetrack in my favorite race car, the TR4. A fitting way to end a very enjoyable eleven-year racing career.

EXPANSION

Further changes to the San Bruno dealership came in 1965. With the business doing well, I was able to buy out Rod Carveth's share in the dealership. When Gyorgy came on board, he contributed to the buyout and in doing so, became a 20% partner in the business. I then received an unexpected phone call from my friend and banker, Clint Luhmann, Senior VP at United Bank of California, which would provide an opportunity for expanding the business further. I remember the conversation, Clint told me one of their clients, a local Mercedes dealer, was going out of business and if he loaned me the money, would I want to take it over? Of course, I said yes. A little trivia here, Luhmann was also Carroll Shelby's first banker and helped him get Shelby American off the ground. As explained later in the book, Clint Luhmann, Carroll Shelby, and I have a few things in common.

I now had my second dealership in just two years, further establishing our presence on the San Francisco peninsula. The new dealership was named Premier Imports of San Carlos, carrying the same lines as the San Bruno store plus adding Volvo. My dealerships continued to prosper, and we were named the top Triumph sales operation in our size category for the U.S. in both 1964 and 1966. Those were great years for my dealerships and for Triumph.

Wasting no time in enhancing my business opportunities, I opened a third dealership in San Mateo also called Premier Imports to sell primarily top-quality used

92 • *Press On... Regardless!*

imports and domestic cars. As a sign of our success, I placed an eight-page advertising supplement in Competition Press/Autoweek magazine timed to coincide with the San Francisco Import Car Show. This in part announced the addition of the third dealership along with my philosophy of running a successful dealership. This is the same philosophy I have had for all these years and still have – people are the key asset of a business, upholding our business policies, our relations with customers, and our longevity. Heavy emphasis is also placed on our parts and service departments, both vital in after sales support.

My appreciation for keeping a car maintained at a high level came from what I learned while racing which I applied to my dealerships. I wanted to build our reputation upon proper treatment of our customers before, during, and after the sale of a car. Doing this successfully would keep customers coming back and enhance the dealership's reputation. Our Service Manager, Curley Welch, was a big part of the reason customers wanted to have their cars serviced at our dealerships. Curley was a gunner on a Torpedo Bomber during WWII and had been rescued from a life raft after his plane was shot down. He and I both worked for Don Hampton, and Curley, who was the Service Manager, prepared my 1962 TR4 race car along with Phil Reilly (yes THAT Phil Reilly). When I opened my second dealership (Premier Imports), I convinced him and the Parts Manager, Ted Lucio, to join me. They were both very honest and capable individuals and that was the beginning of how we conducted business with our customers and continue in our dealership to this day. Curley was with me for 30 years, finishing as Senior VP in charge of three service and parts departments and Master Mechanic. Curley was so humble he didn't know how talented he was. Lucio worked for me for 20 to 25 years.

OPTIMIZING THE BUSINESS

In the early 1970s, Volvo had become a particularly good selling car for us, so I decided to open up a single brand dealership in a new location in nearby Burlingame. Combined with the San Carlos operation, the new store, called Burlingame Volvo, soon became the fifth largest Volvo dealer in the United States for four straight years.

One of the perks provided by Volvo was an all-expenses paid trip for selected U.S. dealers. Our itinerary included stops in Sweden, Norway, Holland, and Denmark, a wonderful and fun trip.

After I became involved with Volvo, I contacted the seven or eight local Bay Area dealers and, with their participation, started the Bay Area Volvo Dealers Association (BAVDA). For a media spokesperson, we were able to obtain the services of Bill Walsh, then the football coach at Stanford University. I had met Tim King, the public relations person for Bill Smythe European, a fellow car dealer and friend of mine. Ergo, I used the name European in my car dealership as a result of our friendship. Tim King had a connection to Bill Walsh's college roommate and Smythe introduced me to him. One thing led to another and Walsh became the BAVDA spokesperson for our television, radio, and print advertisements. When he became the 49ers head coach, he continued with us, inviting us to all the home games, parties, and the Super Bowl. He also was the spokesman for the St. Francis Yacht Club's America's Cup effort (which I was a significant part of), a fruitful relationship that spanned several years.

Bill Walsh, my wife Ellen, and me after the Super Bowl XVI win and predicting the next win (it didn't happen). Bill Walsh was a spokesperson for our BAVDA and later the StFYC America's Cup effort

As sports car sales in general begin to decline in the late 1960s, I decided to sell the San Bruno operation and focus on our other stores. I maintained the San Carlos operation but moved it to another location nearby which had a larger used car lot and a body shop.

Another opportunity came my way in 1982 while I was on a cruise with a friend, Bob Thomas, from Tulsa, Oklahoma (see Ch. 12 Reflections). We were headed to Seattle, then on to Alaska. While on the trip, we docked at Nanaimo on Vancouver Island when I received a phone call from my service manager, Curley Welch. He said that Andy Asbra, the owner of the Jaguar Store (close to my Volvo store) called to say he was selling the business and knowing I liked Jaguars, would I be interested in buying the business? I told my service manager to tell him absolutely yes, I would buy it.

I acquired the property and secured a loan to acquire the Jaguar franchise along with the dealership building with Asbra providing the financing. Not long afterwards, I was offered the Aston Martin franchise and in 1985 I took on Land Rover, which would prove very fortuitous in the long term. The Jaguar, Aston Martin, Land Rover lineup proved to be quite successful, and the dealership prospered.

JAGUAR CALLS

In 1987, Jaguar's popularity was on the upswing and our solid relationship with Jaguar's HQ on the East Coast was about to pay a big dividend. Mike Dale (a former SCCA National Champion), the President of Jaguar USA, called and said, "We have a dealer not doing well in Walnut Creek and Oakland so we would like you to take over both locations and move the whole operation to Walnut Creek eventually." To help facilitate the changeover, Jaguar offered $1000 for every sedan sold if I would match it to develop a kitty to buy the dealer out. I accepted this proposition and when the present owner closed the Oakland

store, I completed the purchase of the Walnut Creek dealership with the help of the kitty.

The number of my dealerships now grew to four, one in San Carlos, two in Burlingame/San Mateo, and the latest one in Walnut Creek. I closed the San Carlos store, moved Volvo in with Jaguar, and sold the Burlingame property and the SAAB franchise to Kjell Qvale. I moved Jaguar to Walnut Creek but maintained a service department in Burlingame at Jaguar's request which I did for about three years. Across the street was Joe Putnam's dealership. Ironically, in 1954, he and I worked for the same car dealership in Minneapolis, mayor Irv Reider's Motor City. In the early 90s, I sold that property and the Volvo franchise to Joe (Putnam) which left me with the one store in Walnut Creek. During this same period, I closed a small leasing company I owned for several years to focus on the single dealership.

With the success of the Walnut Creek dealership, a more modern facility was needed, so in 2016, a new sales building for Jaguar and Land Rover was constructed in the same location and replaced the older facility. Five years earlier we had built a new, state of the art service facility with 30 computerized service stalls not far from our

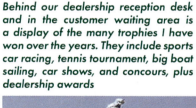

Behind our dealership reception desk and in the customer waiting area is a display of the many trophies I have won over the years. They include sports car racing, tennis tournament, big boat sailing, car shows, and concours, plus dealership awards

96 • *Press On... Regardless!*

new sales building and have been ranked number one in Jaguar service and parts for Northern California. As of 2022, Cole European has been in Walnut Creek for 35 years and has become an institution in the area with a well-earned reputation for quality cars and excellent customer service. We are also the number one dealer for Jaguar and Land Rover for Northern California.

SPECIAL PEOPLE

WAYNE BABCOCK

Wayne is my General Manager and a partner in the Jaguar/Land Rover dealership in Walnut Creek. Someone must be responsible for providing the wherewithal to support the activities on a daily basis described in this book. He is that individual and has been with me for over 30 years. I have a lot to be thankful for and he is among those who deserve the credit. Press On!

BRIAN GUIER

Brian is the General Sales Manager of Cole European and he also has been with Wayne and me for over 30 years. He is certainly among those deserving of my thanks as he continues doing his job in an extraordinary manner. Brian, along with Wayne, make a true team with which I am very pleased to be associated. Press On!

RICHARD BEATTIE

Richard is a Brit and was the Senior Vice President of Jaguar. With his British accent, he called Michigan, "Mikey-gen," and people were "peeps," which always amused me. Richard was by far the best, most capable dealer representative I worked with in all my years in the car business. He was superb and really cared for the dealers. He went to bat for us several times and was instrumental in supporting me and my way of doing business even during the bleak periods when things were not going so well for my company. He bucked company policy when he approved of our splitting our service and sales departments into two separate entities. I have a lot of people to be thankful for who helped my dealerships and me be successful, and Richard is right there at the top. Thank you, Richard.

CLINT LUHMANN

Clint was the Senior Vice President of United California Bank (UCB) in charge of all automobile dealer relationships. I met Clint at the Casa Munras Motel in Monterey, California, in the early 1960s, where we often stayed during the race weekends at Laguna Seca as it was headquarters for the SCCA. We began a friendship that is explained in another chapter of this book. Clint was also a graduate of the U.S. Naval Academy and, as is the custom, each graduate receives a deck watch (clock) which is quite suitable for celestial navigation. Clint gifted said "watch" to me, for use with the sextant, on my first Transpac race to Hawaii in 1975. It is presently displayed on my desk at home. He was quite instrumental in the progress of my business and for that and his ongoing friendship, I am very thankful.

Clint managed all the relationships with the car dealers, a very important part of the bank's business and we developed a very good business and personal relationship. I remember a phone call I received from him one day, a call which caught me by surprise. Clint told me he had to offer his portfolio to other banks due to a major financial issue which had occurred in another area of his bank. He wanted to know if I knew of other banks that might be interested in taking on this business. I gave him a few contacts I felt I knew including Walt Fulton of the Bank of America, and he thanked me and concluded the call. Not long after that conversation I received a call from an officer of the Bank of America who told me he was now managing our account and thought it would be a good idea for us to meet! Can you imagine this happening today?

WALT FULTON

Walt was a Senior Vice President of the Bank of America and the head of its massive Timeplan Loan Department. I don't recall the exact date I first met him, however our relationship developed over the years and became quite close. He was a member of the Olympic Club in San Francisco and he and I played golf there many times. A windbreaker he gave me with the Olympic logo I still wear to this day. After he retired, he often visited me at The Candy Store for a chat and lunch. When the new B of A building was opened, Walt invited Ellen and me up for dinner on the top floor with a tour of his office and environs. Truly a wonderful man with a prodigious memory and admired and beloved by the many who knew him. I remember him with fondness and great respect.

The Candy Store, an ex-Cadillac and Packard dealership building, classic architecture inside and out

Press On... Regardless!

– CHAPTER EIGHT –
THE CANDY STORE STORY

It was in 1977 that I first met Russ Head (later to become the co-founder with me of The Candy Store) at the Palo Alto Concours on El Camino Real. He was polishing the SU carburetor on his recently acquired Jag XK 120. For whatever those ethereal reasons were, we struck up an immediate simpatico and began meeting for the occasional lunch – most often at the then Hyatt House world headquarters in Burlingame. Since we had both just begun what was to be our long-time odyssey with collector cars – we both lived in Hillsborough – and our garages (mine was a triple carport), were filling rapidly – we began the thought process of how to relieve our mutual dilemmas by securing – somewhere – a garage site whereby we could increase our shared mutual addiction with others of similar needs. We expanded our intentions to include our several acquaintances, who undoubtedly needed their own "relief" from similar miseries!

Russ almost immediately found a warehouse near his office, on Burlway in Burlingame near the San Francisco Airport. It was one-fifth of a building, and we could occupy it for only a one-year lease! Ergo – we had a place! At one of our luncheons at the Hyatt House, we forged the name The Candy Store from personal experiences. Interestingly, I was born in Evanston, Illinois, and Russ was from most recently Chicago, where The Candy Store was some sort of emporium or theater.

In my reminisces about growing up in Minneapolis, Minnesota, there came to mind a corner drug store. Upon entering on the right, there was one of those long-slanted glass cases loaded with all sorts of candied confections and delectables. I could recall being mesmerized by their attractions and seemingly had to have one of each! – (echoed later by the ethos of The

Candy Store) – we had a name: "The Candy Store!"

We occupied the warehouse, and to defray expenses I moved my leasing company and personal office into the new digs and Russ, as an investment banker, moved in some of his office activity as well.

We were confident that there were many like-minded enthusiasts on the Peninsula who would gladly like to store their precious collector autos in our newly found garage and, for a modest and very reasonable fee, rent spaces from us. We were quite surprised that there were so few takers! The idea promulgated was plenty of space to park your driver and take your collector car out for a run as a member of a fledgling club, The Candy Store, to which we gave the nickname of SOMA – "Society of Mutual Addiction."

At any rate, it took a piece of time to fill the space with appropriate cars and owners, and the parties and events began! We were there some 3.5 to 4 years, and in that period the club became very viable and active. But alas our lease was up, and we had to find another place.

To our good fortune, we were made aware of our present location and that the current tenant was moving. It had previously been a Cadillac dealership, and was built and occupied in the 20s as a Packard dealership. So, Russ and I guaranteed the lease for several years and this little club, with very few assets, continued as it formalized into a corporation – The One East Lane Corporation.

My upstairs office in The Candy Store

We had several meetings at the Bombay Bicycle & Riding Club, the English Pub – (The Bit of England), and Russ's home. About 18 to 20 members joined in forming the new corporation that is now in its 40th year!!! We adopted a slogan that read: "Great Cars – Good People." We deliberated long and hard about not calling ourselves "Great" as it seemed somewhat elitist, and we felt we were somewhat insignificant at the time. Somewhere along the way it was altered – I'll leave it to others to assess the efficacy of that appellation. Nevertheless, through all these years there has been an unaccountable number of world rank collector cars in this house of ours. I take great pride in the impressively high level of talent, expertise, accomplishment, and caliber of the current Candy Store membership. Press on!

CHANGES AND GROWTH

The building had two offices above the former car showroom and service area, so Russ took one office for his investment banking business. In about 1985 or '86, he moved his office to San Francisco, and I paid him for the improvements he had made and his part of the lease. I then made the upstairs area the main business office for my three dealerships and a small leasing company I had started.

Membership in The Candy Store was based on availability of storage space for cars. Over the years our regular membership has fluctuated between 30 and 40 but it took some time to get to that level. The Candy Store is selective about who can join since we want a group of members with broad interests (i.e. not too many racers, motorcyclists, pre-war car owners, etc.). In recent years, members' interests have been shifting from older cars to more modern cars as more younger members join. This is a similar situation which has confronted other car groups and vintage racing organizations. In addition to the regular members, there currently are associate memberships which number around 60 to 70. They have the same access to the building and activities, but cannot store a car(s) or vote.

Activities have always centered around social gatherings, but the newer members have been organizing a once-a-month tour

With my longtime friend Leon Mandel   *With Carroll Shelby at The Candy Store*

of area roads. However, these have turned into a rally populated with mostly newer cars. This is a disappointment to me as I would like to see more older cars, which is what the club was founded for. In the early years of The Candy Store, we were very proud of the great cars our members displayed/stored at our facility. As I said, our motto then was "Great Cars and Good People." But where have the great cars gone? Are they now relegated to being Garage Queens? With the change in times our motto now could be "Good Cars and Great People." It is readily evident that many members can have their own facilities for their cars (as I do). However, I rotate my cars for display at The Candy Store and wish others would do the same. For example, the Academy of Art University in San Francisco continually displays some of its magnificent car collection at The Candy Store. Perhaps others should follow their example. Again, a parallel situation facing other clubs. I have attended a few of our rallies, but I am not a regular participant since I would prefer them if everyone drove older cars, let alone being old myself!

Another activity was the once very popular Second Tuesday Speaker Series which lasted for about 20 years, but is no longer held on a regular basis. In its heyday, the Speaker Series had a number of high-profile guest speakers including Bob Lutz, Stirling Moss, Carroll Shelby (above right), Jackie Stewart, Dan Gurney, Leon Mandel (above left), and Denise McCluggage. Now there are only occasional special events like Joe Brillando's and now Colin Bach's annual Ferrari Night where an F1 expert presents an overview of the upcoming Formula One season. There is an annual members meeting, the board meets every month, and the annual Christmas party.

Over the years, I have stored/displayed many of my cars at The Candy Store. These included cars from pre-WWII to more modern classics with most being of British, German, or Italian manufacture. I encourage our members to display their best cars in The Candy Store on a rotation basis. This is an ongoing attempt to keep the display top notch and interesting for members and visitors alike. ★ **REMEMBER, THE CARS ARE THE STARS!**

Since its inception forty-four years ago, The Candy Store has gained visibility around the world that few, if any, other organizations of this type can claim. In addition, The Candy Store has inspired the creation of several other similar car storage/clubs not only in California but around the country.

THE COLLECTOR CAR BUSINESS

Building a collection of interesting and valuable cars came naturally to me, an interest that began with the purchase of my first car at 16 years old. During my college years, this interest turned from domestic to foreign sports cars which lead to amateur racing. Being involved in the car dealership business heightened my involvement selling many different brands which increased awareness of the broad spectrum of old and new cars alike.

Collecting cars was an extension of my interest, enthusiasm, and experience with cars, and even though I did not know it at the time, my collection began with the purchase of a new car over 58 years ago. On a trip to England to visit the annual Earls Court Motor Show in 1964, a new model on the Lotus stand caught my eye, a Lotus Cortina Mk 1 SE. After learning more about the Cortina from Lotus founder Colin Chapman, I ordered one on the spot. Interestingly, I bought it not to sell to a customer but with the intention of keeping it. As the years went by the Lotus Cortina remained in my possession and is part of my collection to this day. Rather a unique vehicle since it is a one-owner car, purchased new and has now been restored by Bob Potts and tuned by Jimmy Griffin, who also worked on it in the 1960s (or when new).

My first collector cars – a Rolls Royce (L) and a Bentley in front of our home designed by Wm. Arthur Patrick, a student of Frank Lloyd Wright. 1953 RR Silver Dawn Long Boot (L) 1947 Bentley "Top Hat" Saloon

As my dealerships grew and became successful, the opportunity to invest in high quality collector cars became more prevalent. However, my first vintage collector car happened by chance and was a reluctant purchase. I received a phone call from a fellow in Canada who said he had a nice Triumph TR1 he wanted to sell. Much as I tried, I couldn't dissuade him from trailering all the way to the Bay Area with his family. When he arrived, I looked the car over. It was OK but I wasn't really interested since overall, the car was hopeless. It had only 64 horsepower to propel the car at full chat. I felt sorry for him after he had driven all that distance with his family, so I couldn't refuse to buy it.

HOBBY TO A BUSINESS

As I began to accumulate a growing number of cars for my collection, it seemed natural to add to my hobby by creating a side business. With my son, Rob, I formed Cole Motor Classics (CMC) in 1987 with the purpose of buying and selling quality collector cars. Those cars were bought and sold separately and did not include any vehicles from my private collection which I accumulated over the years.

CMC was located in a 5000 sq. ft. building close to The Candy Store and was enough of a business to pay the bills and make some money over the ten years it was in operation. We sold a variety of cars including Ferrari, but did not indulge in race cars. Our primary focus was on classic road going cars.

A SPECIAL OPPORTUNITY

In 1989, I received a call from the Aston Martin Factory who asked if I could assist in handling a few historic race cars for the upcoming Monterey Historics. Aston Martin had been designated as the honored marque for the event to celebrate its 1959 World Sports Car Championship and victory at the Le Mans 24 Hours. They would be shipping cars from their museum collection in England – not just any cars, but several of their most significant and prized race cars. I had developed a good working relationship with Aston Martin as a dealer and since we were not far from Laguna Seca, we were the logical ones to support the factory effort. Those rare and valuable cars were received at San Francisco International Airport and delivered to the CMC building in Burlingame for storage until needed at Laguna Seca Raceway...that is, all except for a car shipped from Paris. I received a call from Southern California explaining they had an Aston Martin ready for pickup, and what did I want to do? Without a map, the British assumed San Francisco and Los Angeles were not that far apart and, in any case, Bob would "take care of it." I had to dispatch one of our trucks to pick up the remaining Aston Martin and deliver it to CMC's building.

Special cars from the Aston Martin Museum stored at Cole Motor Classics prior to shipping to Laguna Seca

Chapter 8 – The Candy Store Story • 107

The cars were all prepared and then delivered to Laguna Seca and displayed in front of a full-size recreation of the 1959 LeMans Pits, complete with drivers' names, painted versions of spectators, and pit boxes. It was quite a display and complemented the appearance of many of the historic drivers from the period including my old friend Carroll Shelby along with Stirling Moss, Paul Frere, Tony Brooks, Roy Salvadori, company President Victor Gauntlet, and company owner David Brown. It really was an honor to have those championship cars stored in our facility. It's not often you get that close to such an illustrious group of people.

The Aston Martin display at the Monterey Historics drew large crowds to see these historic race cars

Special guests of Aston Martin and former drivers Paul Frere (L), David Brown (Ctr), and Sir Stirling Moss (R in white shirt)

– CHAPTER EIGHT –
PHOTO GALLERY

Above: We had many distinguished guest speakers at The Candy Store over the years including Sir Stirling Moss

Left: The Candy Store created a foundation of which I was the founding donor

Top: A portion of The Candy Store members' cars on display in the former Packard Car dealership service area

Below: Ferrari 400 SA Short Wheelbase I displayed on the floor at The Candy Store

Chapter 8 – The Candy Store Story • 109

Two of the many guests present at the 1989 Montery Historics that honored Aston Martin were the company president Victor Gauntlet (L photo) and former factory driver, Carroll Shelby (R photo). Both were good friends of mine

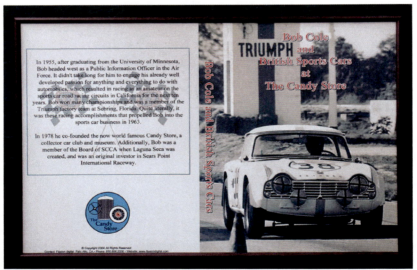

Hanging on the wall of The Candy Store Library is this framed photo with text. It was presented to me by the members after I gave a presentation on my racing career. Photo is of my TR4 team car at Sebring Florida 12 Hour in 1963

A Lady's Reflection

Men indulge in a ritual I find intriguing. It involves their standing around, preferably on concrete (sometimes beaten earth) staring at pieces of things as if they were looking into a ceremonial fire. Often the pieces of things are metal, but sometimes wooden. The pieces belong to something that the men see whole, eyes glazed, as they move in and out of silence. Perhaps they see in those pieces what their primal fathers saw staring into fire.

Men engage in this ritual, mostly in garages or backyards while dinner heats past its prime in off-stage kitchens, or when company is expected momentarily. In turn, the men stir from their reverie, point and talk - sometimes in hushed tones - sometimes in animation — then all lapse again into silence, their gaze on the bones of the thing before them. The car, the boat, the model, the world.

To the casual observer the men are doing as close to nothing as a standing person can do, but don't judge too hastily. And if you are the one with dinner on the stove or plumping sofa cushions for impending visitors, approach these men fastidiously: It's as close as they can come to being pregnant.

After speaking at the Candy Store, Denise McCluggage sent me this short note

Above: Jaguar SS 90; below: 1950 Aston Martin DB2, first DB2 ever delivered

Press On... Regardless!

– CHAPTER NINE –

COLLECTOR CARS

I've been fortunate to own many significant cars with interesting owners and/or history. They have included the ex-Bruce McLaren 3.8 litre Jaguar XKE Lightweight, 2GXO (purchased from the Harrah's Collection); the 1936 Gurney Nutting Rolls Royce Continental MK2 with twin spare tires (now owned by Bernie Eccelstone); and the 1938 Earls Court Jaguar SS100 prototype and show car. This was Sir William Lyons' personal car which was restored in Norwich, England, by renowned Jaguar restorer David Barbour and won the prestigious Montagu of Beaulieu Trophy at Pebble Beach. Of the 1950 Aston Martin DB2 Vantage Coupes manufactured, the first nine were rally and race cars, the tenth was a convertible for David Brown, the eleventh was a factory coupe, and my car (serial number 5012) was the twelfth and the first of its type sold to a customer. Other cars include the 1964 Special Equipment Lotus Cortina (SE); 1963 Morgan Plus 4 Plus Coupe, one of only

1937 Squire

Top: The 1910 Kline-Duesenberg Board Track Racer outside my shop. It won an award at the Monterey Historics and the Pebble Beach Cup at the Concours; middle: Chrysler d'Elegance (promotion photo); bottom: Triumph TR250K Prototype

The 1952 Chrysler d'Elegance Concept Car, a class award winner at Pebble Beach Concours

26 made; 1968 Triumph 250K Sports Car Prototype designed by Pete Brock; the 1937 Squire with Anzani DOHC and supercharged engine, 20" wire wheels, Alfin Brake Drums and Wilson Pre-Selector Gearbox. It was one of nine cars built. I've owned 18 collector Bentleys over the years including both Babe Barnato's legendary 1930 Blue Train Bentley and his 1930 Blower Bentley.

1952 CHRYSLER D'ELEGANCE CONCEPT CAR

The Hemi-powered 1952 Chrysler d'Elegance designed by Virgal Exner with Ghia was a beautiful car and ahead of its time as concept cars are meant to be. It reminds me of a Karmin Ghia on steroids! A friend of mine (John Hopfenbeck, an international car broker) was contacted by another broker who found the car being driven around by an old fellow in the Southern California desert. I bought the car and sent it to restorer Stu Laidlaw in Angels Camp, California, with a short deadline for completion so it could be entered at Pebble Beach.

My friend Gene Babow was able to get a copy of the original plans for the car from Chrysler Heritage which of course was big help during the restoration. Laidlaw did a remarkable job and completed the project in six months, an amazing feat considering the condition the car was in when he started. He had to hand craft from scratch many parts including a new grill, bumpers, and the hydraulically operated, hinged spare tire articulated arm that helped remove the tire from its mounted position. The result was quite stunning, and the car drew quite a bit of attention, received many positive comments, and won a trophy during the concours. This is still one of the most sought-after examples of a concept car.

THE KLINE-DUESENBERG

Over the years, I've owned several significant cars with interesting back stories. This Kline was very special with one of only three such racing engines built by Duesenberg, designed for racing on board tracks. In 1910 Kline built a chassis which was later paired with a 1916 Duesenberg 4.9 litre, four-cylinder, twin under-head cams with double walking beams (eight on each side), 16 valve system, magneto ignition, and a Miller updraft carburetor. Other walking beam engines only had eight valves and eight walking beams while this one had 16 valves and 16 walking beams. The walking beam was a design which essentially was a vertical rocker shaft with the camshaft at the bottom of the engine. The walking beams were vertical rods which actuated the valves on top of the

Top: The unrestored Kline-Duesenberg arrived in pretty rough condition

Left: The connecting rod piston and rocker arm for the Duesenberg "Walking Beam Engine" (photos by Phil Toy)

Curley Welch overseeing the restoration in Stuart Laidlaw's shop

engine when moved by the under-head camshaft. The idea came from Duesenberg himself, an engineer who, when traveling on a transatlantic ocean voyage, saw the ship's engines in operation and applied the design to car engines.

The Kline-Duesenberg won many races in its time before disappearing. Years later, the car was found in a barn in Virginia by a broker from England who bought it, then sold it to another broker in Southern California, who then sold it to me, sight unseen, while it was still in transit from Europe. It was basically in kit form when I received it, so I sent it to Stu Laidlaw to have the car restored with the engine going to Phil Reilly to be overhauled.

The goal was to have the car ready for the 1989 Pebble Beach Concours. It was almost finished when it was shipped to Pebble Beach with just a few minor items to complete. Time was short so it had to go with the hope it could be made ready to display at the Concours. Unfortunately, and despite everyone's best efforts, the car would not start and it was later found that the magneto hadn't been installed properly.

To move the car for display, the only solution was to ask for volunteers to apply some muscle. Fortunately, an illustrious "crew" stepped forward which included Carroll Shelby, Victor Gauntlet (President of Aston Martin), my dealer service manager Curley

Sharing the Monterey Historics with Curley Welch and Bob Potts in the paddock at Laguna Seca

Welch, Bob Potts, and myself. We pushed the car from in front of the Pebble Beach Lodge to our spot among the other Competition Class cars. Bob Potts, one of the "pushers," has been a constant friend for 35 years and is dubbed the "King of Mini-Restorations." No one who I know of can "minimally" restore a classic car to such high standards as Bob.

The following year at the 1990 Historics, we had a much better weekend as you will see in the next chapter. The car was prepared, and I tested it at Sears Point Raceway then had it transported to Laguna Seca for the Historics. After that very successful weekend (one trophy at the Historics, the second, the prestigious Pebble Beach Cup at the Concours), my son, Rob, took the Kline to the big swap meet in Hersey where he sold it to a gentleman from Germany. Sam Mann eventually bought the car and had it shipped back to the US, where it remains in his magnificent collection today.

There is a side story to the Kline which involved a piece of hardware that came with the car when I acquired it – a trophy originally won in a race by the Kline Racing Team. One of my friends knew about the trophy and wanted to buy it, so he paid me a visit. After some negotiation, I sold it to him with the understanding he would split anything over the selling price. He then gave the trophy to a well-known Duesenberg collector presumably in exchange for the opportunity to offer several of the collector's cars at an auction. I haven't heard from my friend since, but I do know that the Duesenberg collector has the trophy.

THE SAGA
OF THE BLUE TRAIN BENTLEY

In the world of classic cars, the story of one of the most legendary cars in the world began with a bet by its owner, the flamboyant playboy, racer, and chairman of Bentley Motors, Captain Woolf (Babe) Barnato. He bet he could drive his Bentley Speed Six from Cannes to London before the famous French Train, the Blue, could cover the distance from Cannes to Calais. Less than 24 hours and 768 miles later, Barnato arrived at the Royal Automobile Club in London several minutes before the French train pulled into Calais. Since then, the Bentley, simply known as the Blue Train, has been one of the world's most sought-after classic cars and one of the most important automotive icons.

I had always admired the Blue Train Bentley after reading about this magnificent automobile and its great history. I told my friend, John Hopfenbeck, "I'd like to own that car one day." John has been a close friend, associate, and collector car advisor to me for the past 35 years. He possesses an unusually encyclopedic memory, which is a valuable asset in the high stakes world of collector cars.

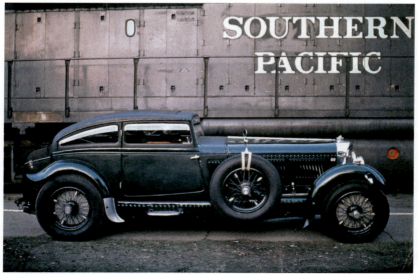

The fabulous Blue Train Bentley was featured in Autoweek magazine in 1985 (photo by Cindy Lewis)

Chapter 9 – Collector Cars • 119

Just So-So Stories

ADD CETERAS: Hillsborough's Bob Cole, who bought the late Babe Barnato's famous 1930 "Blue Train" Bentley at auction in London for 246,000 pounds, will race it against the S.P.'s 10 a.m. run from here to Burlingame station tomorrow — all this to plug the Hillsborough Concours d'Elegance at Crocker School May 19. Barnato raced the Blue Train from Paris to Calais in 1931 and won easily. Cole should do the same...

★ ★ ★

Left: "One more time Natasha"

Since the Blue Train rarely changes hands, I thought I would never have a chance of seeing it again, and that I would have to be satisfied with my knowledge of the car. However, while on vacation in Hawaii in 1984, John found out the car was up for auction at Sotheby's in London. After returning home from Hawaii, and as the date for the auction moved closer, I made arrangements to be on the telephone with one of Sotheby's representatives, Natasha, to place my bids. I anxiously listened as the final bids were coming in for the Blue Train Bentley. I said, "One more time Natasha," and I won, I had the winning bid... the dream car was soon to be in my hands. I found out later the under bidder was none other than my longtime friend Don Williams of The Blackhawk Collection! We didn't know we were bidding against each other.

After clearing the car with British Heritage, (they didn't want the car to leave the country), I had the car shipped via Flying Tiger Airlines to San Francisco Airport where upon arrival and unloading, the Blue Train Bentley was greeted by myself, a group of friends, and members of the press. The arrival of this famous car even made it into Herb Caen's column in the San Francisco Chronicle on January 4, 1985. Caen wrote, "Now then, one of the most famous motorcars in the world – 'The Blue Train Bentley' so-called because it raced the Blue Train from Cannes to London in 1930, winning easily – is about to arrive here. Bob Cole of Hillsborough, the Jaguar dealer and car collector, bought the beauty last month for 246,000 pounds

The Friday Caenicle
★ ★ ★ January 4, 1985

NOW THEN: One of the most famous motorcars in the world — "The Blue Train Bentley," so-called because it raced the Blue Train from Cannes to London in 1930, winning easily — is about to arrive here. Bob Cole of Hillsborough, the Jaguar dealer and car collector, bought the beauty last month for 246,000 pounds ($281,670) at a Sotheby auction in London — one of the highest prices ever paid for a car — and thereby hangs an angle or two ... The car, a 1930 Bentley Silent Speed Six two-door coupe, was originally owned by Joel Wolff (Babe) Barnato, then chairman of Bentley. The late Babe, a millionaire swinger, was hot news around here a few years later when he married a dark-haired beauty named Jackie Quealy and whisked her off to London. The news became hotter when Jackie dumped him to marry her childhood S.F. sweetheart, yachtsman Arvid Norman. When Arvid died, his berth at the St. Francis Yacht Club was inherited by — Bob Cole, the new owner of Babe Barnato's old car.

★ ★ ★

($281,670) at a Sotheby's Auction in London...and thereby hangs an angle or two... The car, a 1930 Bentley Silent Speed Six, two-door coupe, was originally owned by Joel Woolf (Babe) Barnato, then chairman of Bentley. The late Babe, a millionaire swinger, was hot news around here a few years later when he married a dark-haired beauty named Jackie Quealy and whisked her off to London. The news became hotter when Jackie dumped him to marry her childhood S.F. sweetheart, yachtsman Arvid Norman. When Arvin died, his berth at the St. Francis Yacht Club was inherited by – Bob Cole, the new owner of Babe Barnato's old car."

FUN WITH THE BLUE TRAIN

As you can imagine, the Blue Train attracted attention wherever I drove it. I displayed it at car shows including the Pebble Beach Concours, took it on several rallies such as the Colorado Grand (with passengers Curley Welch, Phil Reilly, and Bob Potts), and thoroughly enjoyed the pride which comes with owning one of the world's great cars.

During the Colorado Grand Tour, I was at a filling station when two Alfas went speeding by. I stopped fueling up and off we went in chase of the Alfas. One, a 2.9 was driven by John Mozart and behind him, a 2.3 driven by Bruce Meyers. The road we were on was in exceptional condition. It looked like it was freshly paved with long sweeping turns. I don't remember seeing another car on it as I sped on and I caught up to them. Bob Potts was in the front

Chapter 9 – Collector Cars • 121

The Blue Train Bentley on the Colorado Grand Tour — me and my friends Curley Welch, Bob Potts, and Phil Reilly

passenger seat and Curley Welch in the back. As I approached Meyers' car, his wife was on her knees facing the rear of the car taking pictures of the Blue Train. Later, she showed me the photos and all you could see was a big grill and headlights of the Bentley bearing down on the Alfa. Every time I see Bruce, he recounts that story and says he couldn't believe we caught up to them.

I was involved with the Hillsborough Concours and to promote the event, I drove the Blue Train with San Francisco radio personality, Jim Dunbar, from the city to The Candy Store. Dunbar had a remote radio setup in the car and was broadcasting live providing commentary on our journey.

In 1992, when collector Bruce McCaw expressed interest in the Blue Train but hesitated, I told him, "Bruce, this will be the most important and significant car in your entire collection. It will be in high demand for shows and exhibitions all over the world." He bought the car, and he has been busy with it ever since. When I last saw him, he told me I was right, that it was the most significant car he owned. The Bentley factory has, on numerous occasions, transported the car and Bruce to the U.K. for cars shows, commercial shots, publicity events, etc.

Driver Bob Cole's TR-4 took top honors in the racing class at the Hillsborough Concours.

Ironically, it was discovered this Blue Train Bentley was not the actual car Barnato raced against the train. I knew something about the Blue Train Bentley I owned wasn't right since Barnato's account of the race, given at the Steering Wheel Club in London, stated he had to change a tire and he only had one spare. Well, my car had two spares so I wasn't surprised when the new information came out about the other car. My suspicions were confirmed when Michael Hayes, a well-known Bentley expert, researched the Blue Train's history and concluded it was built after the actual race with the train. Barnato used another Bentley in the race with the Blue Train, which Bruce McCaw located, acquired, and had fully restored. He then displayed both cars at the Pebble Beach Concours.

Co-driver Phil Hill and me with the Blue Train Bentley on the Colorado Grand (photo by John Lamm)

Chapter 9 – Collector Cars • 123

THE OTHER CLUB

For the past ten years, I have kept a handful of my remaining car collection at my shop, which I named "The Other Club" inspired by Winston Churchill's "Other Club" that he cofounded in 1911 along with his friend P.E. Smith. The Other Club is a British political dining society which continued after Churchill's death. My shop is located a few miles from The Candy Store which offers a quick drive between the two locations. It consists of enough storage area

124 • *Press On... Regardless!*

1957 Maserati 3500 prototype – Paris show car

to house several cars, a conference table, and an office upfront at the shop entrance. It's more of a "Man Cave" than an actual shop. Bob Potts has a working shop next door, which is very convenient when I need assistance with anything.

I have a nice collection of photos, memorabilia, Pebble Beach awards, books, and large banners on the walls with pictures of cars from my collection. I don't get to the shop as much as I used to, but I always enjoy my time there when I come for a visit.

I still enjoy buying and selling when a good opportunity or car I am interested in becomes available. In fact, I have recently sold three of my cars at auction and have acquired a very special 1957 Maserati 3500 GT Touring which was the prototype and one of four made. It was shown at the 1958 Paris Auto Show and spent 26 years

1939 Bentley 4 ¼ "overdrive" coupe – one off, built for the chairman of Park Ward Coachbuilder

Chapter 9 – Collector Cars • 125

in the Maserati Museum. With its 3.5 Liter detuned race engine, dual overhead camshafts, and dual ignition, it is exciting to drive and very comfortable as well which is a key consideration at my age!

In addition, I recently acquired from an auction at Amelia Island, Florida, a very rare and special Bentley. The car is a 1939 4¼ Litre Sports Coupe with coach work by Park Ward, known as the "Honeymoon Special," the only one of its kind with wonderful history. This is the 18th Bentley I have owned and a very unique one.

Looking back on my seventy years of involvement with cars of all types, it has been a wonderful hobby/business, and I've made many lifelong friends along the way.

SPECIAL PEOPLE
JOHN HOPFENBECK

John and I have been very close friends since around 1978. He is a constant exponent of positivism – always looking and commenting on the brighter side of all matters – a definite panglossian individual and a delight to be around. He is certainly one of the brightest individuals I know and has helped me acquire many important collector cars. He and I shared offices upstairs in The Candy Store for many years. He is a well-established international broker for collector cars and planned and conducted some 20 plus major car rallies in the U.S. His massive collection of collector books is quite impressive. He is widely known and respected in his field, and it has always been my pleasure to be his friend. We have forged an excellent working relationship from the Blue Train Bentley to the latest, the 3500 Maserati GT Prototype and the Bentley 4 1/4 Litre Overdrive. He is a member of the virtual clubs – The Tangled Web Society and The Other Club, both of which have emanated from my febrile mind. Additionally, he has been of great assistance in the production of this book. Let's hope we all have a bit of panglossianism in us!!

BOB POTTS

The King of the Mini-Restoration, a title I dubbed him with many years ago. He has the rather unique talent of taking an important collector car that needs help and, without actually restoring it, bringing it to "display only" status with remarkable results. He may take a little longer than one expects, but the results are always there. A high recommendation for his talent comes from no less than J. Heumann, the collector car impresario extraordinaire. For years J. had Bob work on his many cars. Before passing, J. bequeathed to Bob several interesting and important items of memorabilia as his way of thanking Bob for all he had done for him. Bob is uncommonly bright and has a degree in agriculture from UC Davis, having grown up on a farm in northern Missouri, a few miles from St. Joseph where my dad was born. Bob also has a longtime relationship with The Candy Store and is, along with Ed Archer and John Hopfenbeck, responsible for the cars' display and care in The Candy Store building. He is very involved with The Candy Store and is a member of the Tangled Web Society and The Other Club.

DON WILLIAMS

Don and I have been very good friends since the late '70s. He, of course, is the President of the Blackhawk Collection and Museum. We very nearly went into business together before the museum was built. Our idea was to combine the sales of contemporary cars with collector cars. It didn't go together but did serve to bond our friendship a long time ago! Since then we have done innumerable transactions in buying and selling collector cars and now that the virus is nearly past, I will again return to my visits at Blackhawk.

Don has graciously let Gary and me meet in his offices at Blackhawk in the writing of this book. He is also a golfer. His wonderful wife, Janet, a few years back, arranged for us to play Cypress Point – still a high point in my golfing memories. Several years ago I encouraged Don to get involved with the Danville Concours – with which Cole European had an ongoing relationship. He did and that union has served everyone well – and provided an avenue of substantially increased charitable revenue for Parkinson's disease.

For the past eight to 10 years we have, through the behest of Don and Janet, been very fortunate and pleased to be ensconced in the room next to theirs at the Pebble Beach Lodge during the Concours. Well, what are friends for? Further, he is Chairman of the Advisory Board (of which I am a member) for the Concours. Don in 2021 celebrated 50 straight years of showing at the Pebble Beach Concours. He has been doing this for longer than I have! Press On! Slot cars, anyone? But that is another story.

Sadly, shortly before going to press with this book, Don passed away. I will cherish the uncountable memories I have of our long friendship whenever they come forward, no matter how often and how reflective they are of our abiding affection for one another. Trust, integrity, and friendship, I would assign to his memory. Thank you, my friend, for being my friend and for allowing me to be your friend. A giant among us has fallen. Alas, parting is, indeed, such sweet sorrow!

CINDY LEWIS

Photographer Extraordinaire! I first met Cindy when the Blue Train Bentley arrived by Flying Tiger Airlines from England in the early '80s. Her glorious works are displayed many times in this book, and it is my additional pleasure that she joins Bob Devlin in selecting the winner of the Bob Cole Award for the Best British Car on the field at the annual Hillsborough Concours d'Elegance! Press On, Cindy, you continue to do marvelous work and always with a smile and a professional determination that is evident in that work. Cindy, you have my admiration, respect, and friendship.

ROY DRYER

Consummate water colorist of great talent and a wit always at the ready to bring joy to the occasion. Roy's images of over some 40 years are amply displayed in this book, both of my cars and my boats. Press On, Roy, and many thanks.

– CHAPTER NINE –
GALLERY – CARS I HAVE OWNED

Top: 1962 Ferrari 400 Superamerica Aerodynamica SWB by Pininfarina
Middle: 1954 Ferrari 250 Europa Coupe by Pininfarina
Bottom: 1962 AC Aceca Bristol

Top: 1954 Ferrari 375 America Vignale Coupe (one of two)
Middle: 1963 Bentley S-3 Continental Flying Spur (one off) Four light Design by H.J. Mulliner
Bottom: 1923 Bentley 3.0 Litre Tourer by Vanden Plas

Top: 1965 Lancia 2.8 Coupe by Zagato
Middle: 1963 Rolls-Royce Phantom V limousine by Mulliner – Park Ward
Bottom: 1939 Jaguar SS 100 Prototype Coupe

Top: 1928 Bentley 6½ Litre Roadster by H. Markham Ltd., one off
Middle: 1957 Jaguar XKSS – one of 16 built
Bottom: 1952 Jaguar XK-120M Roadster

Top: 1923 Bentley 3 Liter Short Wheelbase Red Label – ex Rod Laver. No. 17 of 100 built, first car to achieve 100mph
Middle: 1935 Bentley 3 1/2 Litre Lightweight Coupe by Bertelli – one off
Bottom: 1955 Lancia Aurelia B20, all "Nardi" modifications

Chapter 9 – Collector Cars • 133

Top: 1953 Bentley "R Type"/Continental Lines by H. J. Mulliner, one of three I have owned
Middle: 1929 Jaguar SS 1 Tourer
Bottom: 1962 Alfa Romeo Giulia Veloce Coupe by Bertone

Top: 1929 Duesenberg "SJ" Disappearing Top Convertible Coupe by Murphy – Best of Show at the Hillsborough Concours
Middle: 1954 Cadillac Eldorado Convertible The New York Show Car, purchased from Alton Walker, founder of Pebble Beach Concours
Bottom: 1963 Aston Martin DB4 GT by Touring

Chapter 9 – Collector Cars • 135

Top: 1928 MG K3 Magnette
Middle: 1960 Alfa Romero SZ Coda Tanda or Round Tail by Zagato
Bottom: 1950 Aston Martin DB2, first one ever delivered to a customer

1963 Ferrari 400 Superamerica SWB Aerodynamica Coupe by Pininfarina

1928 Bentley 6 1/2 Litre Road Roadster by H. Markham Ltd

1935 Bentley Kellner coupe

1935 Bentley R Type Continental by H. J. Mulliner

Bentley S-1 Continental DHC by Park Ward

1964 Jaguar 3.8 Mk II Saloon "Rallye Spec"

1972 Volvo P1800 Coupe by Frua (never restored!)

Chapter 9 – *Collector Cars* • 137

Top: 1962 AC Aceca Bristol Coupe
Bottom: Cooling the SS 100 Jaguar engine on the Colorado Grand Tour

Top: 1962 Lotus Elite Special Edition first place, National award winner
Middle: Ellen and me in the Jaguar SS 100 Prototype Coupe (L) leading the SS 100 reunion parade lap at Laguna Seca
Bottom: 1971 AC 428 Convertible

Chapter 9 – Collector Cars • 139

Top: Lotus Indy 500 Turbine Car
Middle: Jaguar XK-150 S DHC
Bottom: An early photo of my British Car collection shown in my driveway at home

Top: Two Bentleys owned by Babe Barnato - the famous Blue Train (right) and the Blower Roadster (left), taken at home in Woodside

Middle: The distinctive rear fender shapes of the two Barnato Bentleys

Bottom: 1973 Porsche 2.7 Carrera "Whale Tail"

Chapter 9 – Collector Cars • **141**

Top: The 4 1/2 Litre "Blower" and the Speed Six "Blue Train" Bentleys both by J. Gurney Nutting
Middle: 1953 Bentley Continental DHC by Park Ward. One of 31 LHD built
Bottom: 1964 Jaguar 3.8 Mk II Saloon Rallye Spec

Top: 1932 Aston Martin 1.5 Litre Le Mans Coupe by Bertelli
Middle: 1930 Bentley 4 1/2 Litre Blower by Vandon Plas
Bottom: 1967 Jaguar XKE 4.2 Coupe Rallye Spec

Chapter 9 – Collector Cars • 143

Top: 1934 Jaguar SS 1 Tourer
Middle: 1961 Jaguar XK 150 3.8 "S" Coupe
Bottom: 1938 Lagonda V-12 Rapide Le Mans Spec Special Roadster by J. Gurney Nutting for the Maharaja of Indore, one off

Top: 1939 Jaguar SS 100 Prototype Coupe, one off (Cindy Lewis photo)
Bottom: 1961 Porsche 356B GT Coupe

Top: 1938 Jaguar SS 100 3 1/2 Litre Roadster
Middle: 1953 Bentley R-Type Continental by H. J. Mulliner (on left); 1958 Bentley S-1 Continental DHC by Park Ward (on right)
Bottom: Ferrari Daytona Coupe

Top: Ferrari Daytona Spyder
Middle: Our daughter Jennifer at her first concours standing beside my 1955 Rolls Royce (longboot) Silver Dawn
Bottom: 1953 Alfa Romeo 1900 CS Pininfarina Berlinetta

Chapter 9 – Collector Cars • 147

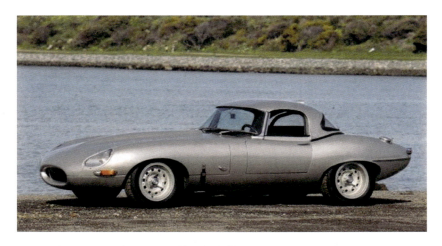

Top: 1965 Jaguar E-Type Lightweight Replica
Middle: 1927 Mercedes Benz "S" Saoutchik Torpedo Brevette
Bottom: 1933 Rolls Royce Phantom II Continental Fixed Head Coupe

Top: 1954 Jaguar XK 120 "C" Drophead coupe, I owned this car three times and still do
Bottom: 1971 Ferrari 365 GT 2 + 2 by Pininfarina at Hillsborough Concours

Chapter 9 – Collector Cars • **149**

Top: My race number represents the number of keys on a piano. I switched to 111 and 112 to meet the SF Region class rules

Bottom: Victory lap with mechanic John Carr at Laguna Seca, 1965

Press On... Regardless!

– CHAPTER TEN –
PEBBLE BEACH

Ever since I visited Pebble Beach and the Monterey area for the first time over sixty years ago, it has remained a special place for me. I have spent many enjoyable days in the area, especially while racing at Laguna Seca and The Monterey Historics, winning best pre-war Alfa Romeo at The Quail, and making many appearances at the Pebble Beach Concours.

THE EARLY YEARS

In 1956, I received my introduction to Monterey as an entrant in my Triumph TR3 at the sports car races at Pebble Beach. This event was unlike any other race I had attended with the large crowds, festive atmosphere, and a course that ran through a forest; it was a great occasion. There was also a concours held at the Pebble Beach Lodge which added another element to the weekend's events. Looking back, I was fortunate to have experienced this combination of racing and classic cars. Pebble Beach was a magical place then and would become a bigger part of my life in the following years.

As described in earlier chapters, I continued sports car racing in 1957, plus I was appointed by Jimmy Orr and Kjell Qvale as the Assistant Regional Executive and head of press and public relations for the SFR-SCCA. In this capacity I was involved with both the club and the Sports Car Racing Association of Monterey Peninsula (SCRAMP) on the Laguna Seca Project which eventually brought a new racetrack to the area. The very successful opening race weekend in November, 1957, drew a huge crowd and was a thrill for all of us who participated in those first races, but particularly for me due to the huge crowd in attendance. All the publicity, which was my job to create, helped to promote interest in the event prior to the race and contributed to the huge throng of spectators numbering 35,000 plus which saw this first race at the new Laguna Seca Raceway.

In 1962 or 1963, the Triumph Competition Department headman, Kas Kastner, called and said he had a pair of new Solex carburetors and an intake manifold he would like me to try on our TR4 at the upcoming race at Laguna Seca. He felt it might provide a performance advantage, so I agreed. When we arrived at Laguna, we fitted the new carburetor setup and then went out to practice. We had some trouble at high rpm, but we thought we had it cured so we ran them in the race. Unfortunately, the engine kept missing and I was running along in 5th or 6th place when the problem cleared up. Now I could really race, and I caught up to Ed Leslie (also in a TR4) who was inches behind Ronnie Bucknum, the leader in an MGB. Coming out of the Corkscrew, Leslie knew I was faster than him, so he waved me by. While alongside Leslie, I gave chase after Bucknum towards turn eight and began to catch him when my engine suddenly lost power and I had to pull off the track. We found out later the carburetors were running too lean, causing the engine to hole a piston which, of course, ended my day. It was a shame because I think I could have won that race. Even though I did not finish, my performance during that race may have influenced Kastner and others to invite me to join the Triumph Factory Team for the Sebring 12 Hour race.

Laguna Seca has an enviable record as one of the oldest and continuously operating racetracks in this country. In 1965, I ran my last race before retiring from the sport and appropriately enough it was at Laguna Seca, finishing first in my class. My mechanic, John Carr, joined me for a victory lap, holding the checkered flag while I waved to the crowd. See photo on previous page.

MORE INVOLVED

The Pebble Beach Concours d'Elegance, is certainly regarded as the top of the mountain world-wide. Emulated by many, but equaled by none. I remember my first visit to the Concours in 1956 when I raced on Saturday at Pebble Beach, then visited the Concours with Jimmy Orr on Sunday. Of course, it was quite a bit different then with fewer cars on display. The crowds were much smaller, and there was only the Lodge, no outer buildings. It certainly was more intimate and casual then. This has obviously changed over the years as the event's popularity has grown so much. I visited the races and

In 2004, a car I entered won this Zarini Trophy in class

A few of the ribbons I've won at the Concours

Concours in Monterey on several occasions in the 1970s along with sailing and becoming a member of the St. Francis Yacht Club in 1972. Then in 1978 I cofounded The Candy Store, so it wasn't until then that I became a regular visitor to events on the Monterey Peninsula.

With my successful, growing dealership organization and after the conclusion of my involvement with the America's Cup in 1987, I became more involved with my car collection by showing many of my special cars at various events. Of course, any serious collector dreams of being invited to display a car at the Pebble Beach Concours and perhaps even winning an award, and I was no exception. I continued buying and selling classic cars, plus adding to my personal collection. Ever since I cofounded The Candy Store, I not only had a place to store my growing collection, but also it allowed me to meet a number of other car collectors, several of whom had entered cars in the Pebble Beach Concours. My involvement with Pebble Beach was about to move to a higher level.

Fortunately, the day came when I received an invitation to display one of my cars at the Concours which was followed by many more appearances over the years. I have shown some thirty classic cars on "the lawn," winning several Zarini class awards and ribbons, including the Pebble Beach Cup, the Lord Montague of Beaulieu Cup, plus the Lorin Tryon award. Between The Candy Store and the Concours, I met and became good friends with many people including the two saviors of the Concours, Lorin Tryon and J. (Jules) Heumann who ran the show for many years.

SPECIAL FRIENDS

Among my car friends via The Candy Store, there were three in particular who encouraged me to enter the Concours – Don

Chapter 10 – Pebble Beach • 153

Williams, Lorin Tryon, and J. Heumann. As our friendships grew, so did my enjoyment of being part of the Concours which became a "must attend" date on my annual calendar.

Lorin and J. made regular visits to The Candy Store to see what I may have added to my collection that would be of interest for the Concours. One such car was a 1911 Rolls Royce Silver Ghost Balloon Car complete with picnic basket. Lorin and J. saw the car and said they had to have the car at the show. They said the same thing when they saw my Chrysler D' Elegance concept car – it had to be in the show, which it was, and it won an award.

In the early 1980s, Russ Head and I rented the same two rooms at the Pebble Beach Lodge for the Concours. After the first

A common sight on our balcony overlooking the green at the Pebble Beach Concours.
Top: Guests are Leon Mandel, Danny Sullivan and son, John Hopfenbeck, Carroll Shelby talking to me, Curley Welch (photos by Roy Dryer)
Bottom: John Hopfenbeck, Bob Lee, Carroll Shelby, me, Victor Gauntlet

couple of years, Russ bowed out, so I took over the two rooms, 100 and 101, which were right behind the 18th green and near the water so we could see all the action. I rented those same two rooms for about ten years. Every Sunday morning about 6:30am, the cars entered the lawn area to be staged and the noise would awaken us. We would watch the cars drive onto the field right under the rooms' balcony. As a result, we decided to make it an occasion and had a breakfast party catered by the company store across the street from the Lodge. We even made up special stickers we would use like invitation only tickets to hand out to our friends to join us. We also arranged for a lunch party, but eventually the Lodge became aware of what we were doing and told us all catering must be handled through them which increased our expenditure considerably.

I remember one year, Carroll Shelby, a frequent guest in our room during the Concours, stayed the whole day. He told me since he was in a legal action against the Ford Motor Company, he couldn't go to the racetrack, but didn't want to be seen at the Concours to avoid having to answer people's questions about the lawsuit. So, he "hid out" in our room enjoying the conversation with our guests who came through that day. Having those rooms, the parties, and our friends present was a grand way to spend the day looking over the cars on display and people watching.

Don Williams started a tradition somewhat by accident about this same time when he would leave his hotel room early in the morning (around 6:30 am) to watch the cars arrive at the Lodge to be positioned on the green. Gradually, many others joined Don for this early morning vigil which became known as the "Don Patrol" and became part of the Concours tradition. Attending the Concours has always been a grand social occasion with an opportunity to visit with old friends, make new ones, and see many of the world's greatest automobiles.

SIGNIFICANT CARS I'VE SHOWN

I've been fortunate to be invited to show several significant cars from my collection at the Concours. The first car was an early 1930s Jaguar Standard Swallow 1 (SS1) coupe followed by a

The Squire DHC

Jaguar SS90 (I have owned two SS100 roadsters and a special coupe). I showed my Jaguar 3.5 Liter SS100 prototype coupe built by Abbey. I have shown several rare and unique cars including the 1937 Squire Drop Head coupe (one of nine built) with a DOHC 1500cc, supercharged Anzani engine, a Wilson pre-selector gearbox, 20" wire wheels, Alfin aluminum brake drums, a car way ahead of its time. The Squire was designed by a brilliant young British engineer, Adrian Squire. I've also, of course, shown the fabulous Barnato Blue Train Bentley, as well as his Blower Bentley and many more.

Morgan at Pebble Beach

156 • *Press On... Regardless!*

After seeing my one-of-a-kind Triumph 250K Prototype designed by Pete Brock and built by Kas Kastner, Lorin Tryon and J. Heumann insisted I bring the car to the Concours. "Bring that car to Pebble Beach," said Lorin. "I'll guarantee you a trophy." I did and was awarded a trophy, but there were only three cars in the class and we each received a trophy!

Another car Lorin and J. wanted at the Concours was my restored 1952 Chrysler d'Elegance Concept Car. As mentioned earlier, this car had been discovered in the Southern California desert by a broker friend of John Hopfenbeck who called me. I acquired the car and had Stu Laidlaw restore it in time for the Concours and was pleased to drive it across the stage in front of the crowd and take home a class award.

When Morgan Motors was honored with a special display in 2008, I showed my 1965 Morgan Plus Four coupe (only 26 were made). The last year I showed a car at the Concours, I chose a lightweight, aluminum body 1935 Bertelli Bentley, two-door, four-seater, 3.5-liter with the chassis built by Bentley (later known as Derby after purchase by Rolls Royce) with no running boards or bumpers. It was a one-off car. The car is owned today by collector Arturo Keller. He also owns my Ferrari "Bumble Bee" with a Vignale body, and The Bob Lee Collection has also acquired five of my former cars.

DOUBLE AWARDS

In 1989, the Kline-Duesenberg was invited to be displayed at the Concours. Unfortunately, upon arrival we couldn't get it started so Victor Gauntlet (President of Aston Martin), Carroll Shelby, Curley Welch, Bob Potts, and myself had to push the car into position on the lawn.

The following year, 1990, the car was ready to go, and I tested the car at Sears Point (now Sonoma Raceway) to ensure it was in top running order. At the Monterey Historic Races, the Kline performed very well as I started 27th and worked my way through the field to finish 3rd despite the fact I had not been in a race car on track since 1965. Thankfully, I had retained some of my old racing instincts and skill.

Chapter 10 – Pebble Beach

The award winning Kline-Duesenberg and trophy on the green at the Pebble Beach Concours

During the first part of the race, every time I accelerated hard, the engine would lose power, but I finally found the problem. The car had a Miller updraft carburetor which required a smoother application of the throttle. I also found the car seemed to actually speed up when I applied the rear brakes (no front brakes on this car) and had to grab the big emergency brake handle to slow the car down. Applying these techniques, I was soon passing car after car as I moved to the front of the field. Based on the car's presentation and performance at the Historics, I was presented with the Monterey Historics Award for Pre-War cars.

Following the races, I was asked to bring the Kline to the Pebble Beach Concours the following day to display it on the lawn.

Phil Hill presenting the Pebble Beach Cup (don't touch that exhaust, Ellen) at the Concours

158 • *Press On... Regardless!*

The car attracted quite a bit of attention from the crowd. Even Paul Frere and Phil Hill, both former Grand Prix and LeMans drivers, were fascinated by the car's unique engine. I was very pleased when the car was awarded the Pebble Beach Cup, after being judged the "Most Significant Race Car" on the field. Making it even more special, my old friend Phil Hill presented me the award on the ramp. Phil was my co-driver in the Blue Train Bentley on the Colorado Grand Tour one year.

Another surprise came at the 1990 Concours when I was fortunate to receive a very prestigious award, the Montagu of Beaulieu Trophy. The Award was presented to me by Sir Stirling Moss which made it even more special. The award is given for the "Most Significant British Car" which in this case was my Jaguar SS100 Prototype Coupe which I had on display. This was a very unique car since it had been Sir William Lyons' personal car.

I had previously purchased a Jaguar SS90 and SS100 from David Barbour. I knew he had this car, which was in his shop in Norwich, England. I knew Barbour had earned a reputation for restoring pre-war Jaguars. Well, it took me two or three years to convince Barbour to sell me the car and restore it to its former glory. As an incentive, I told him I would fly him and his wife to attend the Pebble Beach Concours when the Lyons SS100 was on display. Imagine his excitement when the car he had restored was awarded the Montagu of Beaulieu Trophy.

SPECIAL INVITATIONS

Even though my friend Ed Gilbertson (Concours Co-Chair and Chief Judge) had asked me on several occasions to become a judge, I told him I did not want to be a judge and show a car at the same time. I finally relented and I was a judge for 15 years and became a member of the original Steering Committee and the now-named Advisory Board.

As an honorary judge I met and grew to be friends with Jack Telnack, Global Vice-President of Design for Ford Motor Company. When Ford bought Jaguar, Telnack formed a small committee to fly over to England to advise them on future designs. Several prominent people were involved including Telnack, Ralph Lauren,

J. Heumann, myself, and one other person whose name I can't recall. Of course, the British Ford designers weren't too happy to have a bunch of Americans come over and tell them how to design cars! However, it was quite an honor to be selected for the committee, and I subsequently received a letter from Telnack thanking me for being part of the committee.

Whether it be as an entrant, judge, or member of the Steering/Advisory Committee for the Pebble Beach Concours, I have thoroughly enjoyed the experience. The Concours is the most prestigious event of its kind in the world and to have been a part of it is an honor in itself.

LORIN TRYON AWARD

Perhaps one of my biggest surprises and a memory I cherish for what it stands for, came to me courtesy of the Pebble Beach Concours in 2019. I was presented with the Lorin Tryon Award which "recognizes an automotive enthusiast who has contributed significantly to the Pebble Beach Concours d'Elegance and the car collector world." The award means a lot to me since Lorin, J., and Don Williams were very special friends whose company I always enjoyed and who helped shape the world's greatest concours d'elegance.

BEYOND PEBBLE BEACH

While the Pebble Beach Concours was my main focus, I did show cars at other events including The Cavalino Classic, Presidio Concours, Silverado, Palo Alto, The Quail, Marin, and Hillsborough Concours. One year at Hillsborough, I showed a 1929 Duesenberg Murphy Convertible Roadster with a supercharged engine and won Best of Show. Ken Bering, who developed Blackhawk, bought the car for the opening of his museum. Ken and Don Williams invited me over for the grand opening and proudly showed me the car on a turntable upstairs. It was the featured car of the night.

I had shown this same Duesenberg at Pebble Beach along with two other Duesenbergs in the class. Each one of us scored the full 100 points, but no ties were allowed so it had to be broken. The cars were rejudged and afterwards, I was awarded third when a judge discovered a very minor flaw in a fender welt, a small ripple in the metal trim around the tire. Later, one of the judges came over to apologize saying, "We had to find something, only one car can win." Hmm… third place with 100 points… that's Pebble Beach!

When I was co-chairman of the St. Francis Yacht Club's America's Cup Challenge, one of our events was a parade in San Francisco to generate interest in our effort. For this occasion, I drove my 1954 Cadillac Eldorado convertible which I had acquired from Alton Walker of Pebble Beach. My passengers that day were my wife Ellen, daughter Jennifer, and the Honorary Grand Marshalls Cyril Magnin and Herb Caen.

I have been involved as a participant and sponsor for the long running Hillsborough Concours going back to 1980 when I won a first in class award with my 1947 Bentley MK VI "Top Hat" Saloon. I beat out Carl Carlsen's Rolls Royce MK1 Drop Head. Then a month later at the Palo Alto Concours, the same two cars tied for first. A judge came back over and rejudged the cars and

Chapter 10 – Pebble Beach • 161

1929 Duesenberg SJ Murphy Convertible Roadster, Best in Show at Hillsborough Concours

found my fuel gauge needle was wiggling when the car was running... suddenly, I took second. I think there was a bit of behind-the-scenes arm twisting in this situation.

Besides winning several other awards over the years, I have sponsored The Bob Cole Award at the Hillsborough Concours for "the car of British origin which most clearly exemplifies the essence – the spirit – the design and engineering of the British Auto World." The first award was presented in 2016 to the owner of a beautiful, highly modified, 1950 Jaguar XK120M which was Phil Hill's race car when he won the first Pebble Beach race.

In addition, and through our dealership, Cole European in Walnut Creek, we have been an ongoing sponsor for the Danville d'Elegance car show for over a decade. We helped the show expand by introducing Jim Edlund, the show organizer, to my longtime friend Don Williams, owner of the Blackhawk Collection and manager of the Museum. Since

The Cole Award symbolizing the "V" for victory gesture made famous by Winston Churchill

its inception, the show has been held in early September and has not only become very popular, but also a huge contributor to the Parkinson Foundation Charity. This disease claimed the life of The Candy Store co-founder Russ Head, so this charity has a special meaning to me.

From the 2014 Danville d'Elegance program, Jim Eklund, Co-Chairman of the event for the previous ten years, wrote the following: "I am sure my thoughts are similar to many others who have been touched by knowing Bob Cole. A gentleman... a man of his word... incredibly honest. He sets the bar pretty high!

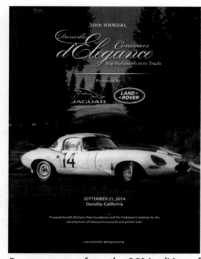

Program cover from the 2014 edition of the Danville d' Elegance.

Bob lost his close friend and Candy Store co-founder Russell Head, to Parkinson's. The day I contacted Bob to become involved with our event he said, "WE'RE in!" That first year our Tour went to The Candy Store. As Bob spoke to the group, I will never forget the emotion in his voice when he talked about Russ.

Cole European supported us from then on. Even when the economy went south, they never wavered. That comes from the man at the helm. Ten years later, Cole European is our largest donor and biggest sponsor ever. Bob has always set the example and that is what makes Cole European such a vital, very successful business in our community."

In 2014, I was presented with the Lee Iacocca Award at the Danville d'Elegance which "honors a person who, over time, has demonstrated an extraordinary dedication to the classic car hobby through vehicle preservations, club participation and one who has unselfishly assisted and encouraged others in perpetuating an 'American Automotive Tradition.'"

SPECIAL PEOPLE

J. HEUMANN

He meant so much to so many of us. Even if that statement is somewhat esoteric, in my experience and memory, no other person could come close to emulate his decades long impact on our understanding of and experiential pleasures derived from our ongoing involvement in what binds us together while we mutually enjoy and participate in this rather addictive devotion to what might be casually referred to as a "hobby." But in reality, it must be regarded as a way of preserving a past that is so very deserving of its survival and therefore preserved! No other individual is so deserving of our thanks as J. Heumann in leading us to those determinations... he showed us the way. I say, Press On!

BOB DEVLIN

He is the unofficial historian for the Pebble Beach Concours (so I say!). He has written two books about Pebble, plus many articles. Currently he is an Honorary Judge, one of the few who are non-commercially involved in the auto world after putting in some 30 years as a class judge. His range of knowledge and experience is extensive and impressive. Interestingly, his wife Betsy's sister is married to a retired U.S. Supreme Court Justice, and they all grew up together. Bob and I enjoy shared experiences as members of the Saint Francis Yacht Club and The Candy Store as well as the Tangled Web Society and The Other Club. Press On, Bob.

ED GILBERTSON

He is past Co-Chair and Past Chief Judge at the Pebble Beach Concours and founder of ICJAG, the International Chief Judges Association Group that promulgate Ed's thoroughly proven and established method of judging a concours. Widely known and highly respected throughout the collector car world, he is a consummate leader and organizer. I've previously said he is one of the most accomplished individuals I know, and that is really saying something. I treasure the relationship with both Ed and his "wing man" wife, Sherry. Of course, Ed is an active member of The Candy Store as well as the Tangled Web Society and The Other Club.

THE "HAS BEENS"

Recently I, along with my two great friends, Don Williams and Ed Gilbertson, were able to find a time in our busy schedules to meet for lunch. As long-time veterans of car collecting and the Pebble Beach Concours, we call ourselves "The Has Beens" in deference to the younger generation of collectors and concours attendees. We met at the Blackhawk Museum and, for several hours, had a wonderful time talking about what else... cars and Pebble Beach. It was a conversation that could have gone on for many more hours, but the time we did spend together was very enjoyable.

Me, Don Williams (C) and Ed Gilbertson (R) (photo by Janet Williams)

– CHAPTER TEN –
PHOTO GALLERY

Top: Rolls Royce Balloon car, 1911
Bottom: Jaguar SS 1 coupe, 1929

Top: Gurney Nutting Lagonda Rapide one off
Middle: 1931 Voisin V-12, only one in existence
Bottom: With my friend and cofounder of The Candy Store, Russ Head by a 1939 Jaguar SS100 coupe one off with three Zarinis awarded that day

Chapter 10 – Pebble Beach • **167**

Pebble Beach Concours d'Elegance

Lorin Tryon (415) 838-5537 • Fax (415) 838-4375 • Res. (415) 831-1851, 461-0921
Post Office Box ~~2489~~ 2167 • ~~San Rafael~~ DANVILLE, CA ~~94912~~ 94526

8/27/90

Hi Boo,
 BELATED CONGRATULATIONS! THE CAR AND THE PILOT WERE GREAT AND, JUDGING BY THE CROWDS DOWN BY 101, THE PARTY MUST HAVE BEEN, TOO.
 HOPE TO SEE YOU SOON.
 BEST,
 Lorin

Top: Aston Martin DB2 at Pebble Beach also won first in class at The Quail
Middle: Note from Lorin Tryon on the Kline Duesenberg winning an award
Bottom: Blue Train Bentley on the lawn at Pebble Beach (one off)

Top: 1929 Jaguar SS 1 Coupe
Middle: 1933 Jaguar SS 90 Roadster
Bottom: 1923 Bentley 3 Litre SS – Red Label – first car to 100 MPH

Top: Jackie Stewart presenting award for 1932 Rolls Royce Continental Mark II Coupe by J. Gurney Nutting one off
Bottom: Babe Barnato's "Blue Train" Bentley and Blower Bentley – both one offs by J. Gurney Nutting

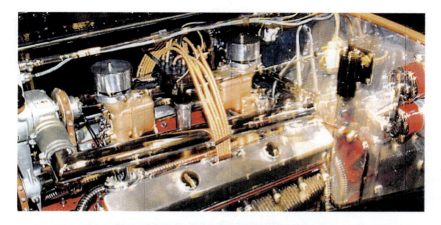

Top: Voisin V-12 Engine – one of one
Middle: 1968 Lotus Elan Mk 2. From a collection in Canada
Bottom: Another one off Bentley! 1935 3.5 Litre "Derby" body by Antem of Paris and originally designed for his personal use by Andre Embiricos – famous for his 4 1/4 streamline Bentley which ran in top ten at LeMans. I've been chasing this car for 20 years – twice it was bought before I could make a bid on it. It remains in the same condition as when I last drove it – the last owner was known for not driving his cars!! After proper "waking up" procedures have been carried out, it will be displayed in the Candy Store

Chapter 10 – Pebble Beach • 171

Above: At the helm of Regardless — an S&S Tartan 41

Main photo: My second sailboat, a 36-foot Columbia, Sea Lotus II

Press On... Regardless!

– CHAPTER 11 –
BIG BOAT SAILING

BIG BOAT SAILING

Since I was raised in Minnesota, the "Land of 10,000 Lakes," the opportunities to become involved in sailing were everywhere. In fact, it's hard to avoid getting involved since sailing is a major leisure time activity during the summer months. My interest in sailing began years ago as a teenager when I attended summer camp after school was out. One summer, at YMCA Camp Iduhapi, I was an assistant counselor to Jim Peterson, who stood about 6' 6" tall and was the University of Minnesota center on the basketball team and a pitcher on the baseball team. Jim asked me to play catch with him one day and introduced me to the curveball, but it had so much spin on it, I could hardly catch the ball. I couldn't believe anyone could throw the ball the way Jim did, let alone control it.

Jim was also a good friend of George Mikan, the former DePaul University All-American and National Basketball Association star for the Minneapolis Lakers. The Lakers eventually moved to Los Angeles in 1961 but retained the "Lakers" as part of their name, thus the Los Angeles Lakers, the first NBA team on the West Coast.

Jim gave me my first set of lessons in how to sail a small boat (16' X Class) on a local lake. During one of my first lessons with Jim as a passenger, we pushed off from shore and I promptly capsized the boat (turned turtle)! We were able to right the boat and, once seated, Jim asked me how far from shore I thought we were. I looked out across the lake to the shore which seemed a fair distance away. Jim said, "Now turn around." When I did, here we were so close to the shore we could have easily swum back to the beach.

These early sailing lessons got me started and I gained more experience with the help of my brother whose friends had a bigger, 30' Class A boat on Lake Calhoun. Actually, I think they took me in primarily to help them sand the bottom of their wooden boat.

My sailing activity was limited since high school, cars, and tennis took up most of my time. After graduating from high school and enrolling at University of Minnesota, my schedule became even busier. School, cars, and joining the U.S. Air Force ROTC were the pursuits where I focused my energy and time, so sailing took a back seat. It wasn't until several years later, and after I moved to San Francisco, that sailing reentered my life and in a big way.

After the U.S. Air Force assigned me to San Francisco, I was focused on fullfilling my military service and sports car racing. I completed my military commitment in 1957 and transitioned to civilian life and the business world. Of course, I continued sports car racing for the next few years enjoying a good level of success, all with Triumph Sports Cars. Then in 1965 and with two car dealerships to look after, I retired from sports car racing after eleven enjoyable years in the sport. Not one to sit around much, I considered other possible hobbies with sailing at the top of my list. With several of my car racing friends also active in the boating community, it didn't take long for them to convince me to get involved, and a short time later I purchased my first sailboat, an older 26-foot Columbia.

Sailing on the San Francisco Bay has many challenges that take time to learn – changing winds, tides, weather, and other boat traffic all require your attention. After gaining experience sailing for fun, I felt it was time to begin entering local boat races. After a few events, I realized the 26-foot Columbia was not very fast, or as I described the boat, "It was a slug." After selling it, I purchased a new design 36-foot Columbia (I named it Sea Lotus) and continued racing, now with a more competitive boat. I ultimately sold it to my friend Al Coppel, an OSCA racer and author of the book *Hero Driver*.

There were many memorable days sailing on the bay, but one race in particular nearly got us into big trouble. It was a windy day on the bay as it often was, and we became dismasted with lines, sails, and part of the mast overboard in the water. To complicate things, our boat was in the path of an incoming oil tanker which was bearing down on us. It was blowing its horn as a warning, so we scrambled to retrieve the items in the water and maneuver to get out of its way, which we were able to do. It certainly was exciting for a while.

I became more involved in my boat and racing, thoroughly enjoying the competition and the social aspect of the sport. Friends

Regardless, crossing the finish line in the 1975 Transpac race. We finished third in class and fifth overall

who were members of the St. Francis Yacht Club — my former car racing friends, Jimmy Orr and Cal Paige, and another good friend, Leonard Delmas – sponsored me, so I joined the club in 1972 and am still a member today. However, just before being accepted into the club, Orr and Paige gave me some excellent advice. I was on my boat motoring out towards the bay when they came running along the quay trying to get my attention. I pulled into a slip where they proceeded to tell me that if I wanted to be in the club, I'd have to shave off my beard and mustache. Otherwise, the club would not approve my application. A bit stodgy wouldn't you say? Well, as soon as I got home, I shaved all of it off and was duly accepted as a member in the St. Francis Yacht Club. This was an interesting expression of the mores extant at the time.

BIGGER BOAT, BIGGER RACES

As my crew and I became more proficient, we began winning races, including the first StFYC Inter-Club Regatta in 1972. Spurred on by this, I set sights on bigger competition and to do so, I bought a bigger and faster boat in 1974, a Tartan 41-footer. The boat

The crew as we approached the finish line at Diamond Head (off Honolulu) in the 1981 Transpac, winning Class A

had been designed by a well-known and respected team out of New England, the brothers Olin and Rod Stephens. I named the boat "Regardless" and with it and good crews, we immediately started winning races including the Big Boat Series in San Francisco Bay. Ironically, my first ever trip to Hawaii was when I raced in Regardless during the 1975 Transpac (the 2,225 nautical mile Transpacific Yacht Race from Pt. Fermin in San Pedro, California, to Diamond Head in Hawaii) where we finished 5th overall... but it certainly wouldn't be my last trip to the islands.

I entered the boat in other races including The Danforth Ocean Racing Series which we won, the San Diego to Puerto Vallarta, the MEXORC Series (Puerto Vallarta to Zihuatanejo), and two Transpacs. I had a scary incident at the conclusion of the Danforth Race as we approached the Golden Gate Bridge on a very foggy night. We were under full sail with the spinnaker up and I was at the helm. I saw a dim incandescent light in the distance, but could not see much else. As it appeared to be heading in our direction, I continued to watch it when suddenly I saw the light was attached to a large cargo ship on a collision course with us. I spun the wheel hard to port, dumping the spinnaker into the water, but we avoided the ship. While trying to calm my nerves, we continued to the finish and won the race. We radioed the US Coast Guard about the incident.

We had good success in these events racing against top competitors including international boats and crews. As a result, Regardless was becoming a well-known boat which helped us attract a number of excellent crew members as time went on. One crewman was a real jack-of-all-trades and was with me on all three of my boats (Sea Lotus, Regardless, and Zamazaan) for all the events I entered. His name was Jim Jessie. He was a very competent sailor, navigator, helmsman, cook – the personification of a sailor. We were fortunate to have him on board in so many races.

Ocean racing is a very different experience than bay or coastal racing. You and your boat are a self-contained life system with a crew (depending on the boat size – in my case up to 11) plus food, water, and other essentials for the number of days of competition. It's quite an experience to be out on the open ocean with nothing but sky and water in sight plus an occasional passing boat during the day, then more stars than you've ever seen at night.

To help on our first Transpac race, my old friend and banker, Clint Luhmann, who was a graduate of the Naval Academy at Annapolis, gave me a beautifully made and very accurate ship's deck clock. This clock is given to cadets upon graduation. Jim Jessie and I used the clock along with a sextant to fix our position during the race and the combination of those two instruments worked very well. I still have that clock on display at my home today.

ZAMAZAAN

After the second Transpac race, something unexpected happened that captured my attention. We were tied up in the docks at Ali Wai Yacht Harbor in Honolulu after the race when I saw a gorgeous boat go by. It was a beautiful fractional rig boat with twin wheels and its image stuck in my mind. A fractional rig on a sailing vessel consists of a

Zamazaan was a great boat in which the crew and I won many big races

Chapter 11 – Big Boat Sailing • 177

foresail, such as a jib or genoa sail, that does not reach all the way to the top of the mast and is very popular on racing boats. This type of sail rigging can provide an advantage in maneuverability around a racecourse.

After returning home to California, I learned the boat was for sale, so I investigated and confirmed it was indeed for sale, but now located in Hauraki Bay, Auckland, New Zealand. It was owned by a well-known architect who had worked for the Shah of Iran. The boat's name was Zamazaan, the same name as a racehorse bred by the Shah. The boat had been designed by Bruce Farr, one of the best-known naval architects and, at 53-feet in length, it was the largest fractional rig sailboat in the world at that time (except for 12 meter and larger boats).

After communicating with the owner, my wife Ellen and I flew to New Zealand late in 1979 to look the boat over. After taking the boat out for a "demonstration sail," I knew it was the right boat for my future sailing endeavors. However, there was a little drama attached to how we acquired Zamazaan due to the owner being in debt, thus his need to sell the boat. There were monies owed to several people and there was group of "vigilantes" who would not allow the boat to leave New Zealand until the debt was paid. This group did not want to see the boat disappear in the night without it being legally free to depart. Back in California, I hired a friend of

I am at the helm with the crew busy trimming the sails. This is typical of the action during a race (photo by Phil Uhl)

mine, Warwick "Commodore" Tompkins, a very experienced and well-known sailor who often ferried boats between destinations for customers. He was highly regarded around the world and was also a great teacher who taught me a lot about all aspects of sailing and boats.

Tompkins flew to New Zealand to make sure Zamazaan was safe, the creditors were paid out of an escrow account held by our attorney, and to prepare the boat for its journey to California. He hired an experienced ocean sailing crew and our new acquisition finally made the long journey to Honolulu where we entered the Pan American Clipper Cup Series. This was an important international event with 67 entrants (see later in this chapter). We stayed in Honolulu for one month, then brought Zamazaan home to San Francisco. We then entered the St. Francis Yacht Club's Big Boat Series where it handily won Class A and the San Francisco Cup.

MAN OVERBOARD

The usual routine before the start of the Transpac race was to sail our boat down to Marina del Rey to gather for the start of the Transpac at Point Fermin near Long Beach. We had the racing crew on board, so the trip was a good test of the crew and boat. One of my watch captains, Skip Steveley, strongly recommended I take on a new crew member who had zero experience with boats or sailing. Steveley said this young fellow was very intelligent, a great athlete, and had recently climbed Mt. Everest! Can you imagine being so competent both physically and mentally to accomplish such a feat? He had even placed a flag from the St. Francis Yacht Club at the top of the mountain. Against my better judgement, I said OK, and this fellow turned out to be a very quick study and an excellent crew member.

On our way down the coast one early morning, the wind had been increasing in strength and we hit rough weather with big waves. I gave the wheel to Jim Jessie so I could get some rest. But before I went below, the boat was lifted onto its starboard side by an unusually large wave. When we righted, the wind would blow us down again. I then realized we had a man overboard who had been standing right next to me. It was Bob Hargis, an ex-marine. Fortunately, he was wearing an orange-colored life jacket. Kim Livingston, boating editor for the SF Chronicle, came up topside, so I grabbed him and said, "You and I are going to keep an eye on Hargis." Jessie locked our coordinates into the GPS and we fortunately weren't moving too far away from Hargis due to the waves knocking us down.

We pulled in the spinnaker and got the mainsail on the correct side of the boat. I sent a man forward with a knife in his mouth to cut the boom vang to allow the mainsail to switch sides, but before he got there, the vang broke and the mainsail rapidly changed sides with the boom slapping the water. I thought it was going to break, but luckily it didn't and also didn't hit anyone. We finally were able to collapse the spinnaker before it blew itself out and we got the boat under control. We started up the 85hp diesel engine and turned the boat around. At this point, the wind was blowing 50 knots as we were rising and falling between the huge swells.

I deployed four crew members to the mid-deck, two on each side at maximum beam, ready to grab Hargis and bring him onboard. We sighted Hargis, but missed getting him twice, so on the third attempt, I pointed the boat right at him. We lowered the lifeline gates, and I knew he would come down one side of the boat or the other. Sure enough, the two guys on the port side grabbed him and pulled him onboard, almost throwing him over the other side. I'll never forget Hargis looking up at me and mouthing the

A good gust of wind can easily knock a large boat, even the size of Zamazaan, over on its keel

180 • *Press On... Regardless!*

words, "Thank you." That was an exciting and somewhat perilous, frightening time and we hadn't even started the race!

We had a couple of bruised crew members and one, Bill Ormond, who had tumbled from his bunk and through the galley, ending up with ruptured spleen and cracked ribs. We headed for Morro Bay to get out of the weather and get our injured crewman medical attention. Sadly for him, he didn't make the trip to Hawaii.

A RACE WITH NO WIND

In the 1979 Transpac Race (known as The Turtle Transpac) with Regardless, the whole fleet was becalmed twice partway across the Pacific Ocean. We went swimming in several thousand feet of water with a rope tied to our waist and attached to the boat since it would drift away with the current. The lack of wind lasted much of 14 days. We almost ran out of water and food, but managed to ration what we had

Below deck, checking our course on the charts, aboard Regardless

and eventually finished the race. That was a close call, but satisfying to have endured and made it to the finish in Honolulu.

SUCCESS WITH ZAMAZAAN

I entered Zamazaan in the 1980 Pan Am Clipper Cup Series, a big international event consisting of five races over three weeks in Hawaii. The series included three buoy races, a long race around the island of Oahu, and a three-day race around the entire chain of islands. I had an excellent nine-man crew flown in for the series including Paul Cayard who was only 19 years old at the time, but destined to became one of top sailors in world. After completing the "around the state of Hawaii race," we finished third boat out of

Chapter 11 – Big Boat Sailing • 181

67. The only two boats in front of us were "maxi-yachts,' 80-feet long. We were the top American boat for the whole regatta and Jim Jessie won the Navigators Award for the series of races, which was well deserved.

After the finish, we tied up at the Ali Wai Yacht Harbor in Honolulu. Jim Jessie came over to me and said, "Give me your watch. You are going into the water." This is an old tradition for a skipper of a winning boat to be tossed into the water. Two crew members picked me up and into the harbor I went. Now I'm in the water looking back up at Zamazaan wondering how I am going to get back onto the boat.

1st in Class Trophy – Pan Am Clipper Cup 1980

Zamazaan – 1980 Pan Am Clipper Cup in Hawaii winning Class A and first American boat in a five-race international regatta

On our way to winning the Big Boat Series with Zamazaan on San Francisco Bay in 1980. Note the boat's fractional rig configuration

Before I knew it, 19-year-old Cayard was in the water next to me. He put his hand on my rear end and shoved me up so I could get back onto the boat.

Having won the Big Boat Series and Pan Am Clipper Cup Series, I now wanted to win the Transpac in Class A. Being somewhat of a student of the rules governing big boat sailing (remember my days as Rules Committee Co-Chairman in the SF Region SCCA), I realized with the solid propeller on Zamazaan, it would most likely classify us at the top of Class B. I decided to install a folding propeller on Zamazaan, which makes the boat faster. This meant I would need to have the boat inspected and rerated. I arranged for the inspection and waited for the results. The data from the inspection was put into a complicated formula and the result showed we were rerated into the bottom of Class A. This now hopefully would give us an edge against the other Class A boats. It did help as we won Class A in that year's Transpac. The old SCCA rules guy strikes again... pay attention, pay attention.

Zamazaan won Class A for the whole series and was the top American boat. In addition, we also won the Big Boat Series in SF Bay and the Transpac Class A, earning the yachting equivalent of the Triple Crown, a feat which has not been duplicated before or since. After such success, I sold Zamazaan to another local yachtsman in San Francisco and the boat is currently moored at the St. Francis Yacht Club. Cayard has been world champion seven times in various classes of boats and recently completed an excellent term as Chairman of the Board of St. Francis Yacht Club. He was recently elected to the Bay Area Sports Hall of Fame, the first sailor to be inducted, and in 2021 he was appointed to lead the U.S. Olympic Sailing Team.

OUT OF COMPETITION

After entering competitive sailing and winning many races, including the Triple Crown, I decided to retire from big boat racing. Instead of a new sailboat, I acquired a 43-foot Cheoy Lee Motor Sailor which was meant for more relaxed family exploration of the San Francisco Bay and surrounding waterways. In addition, it was the St. Francis Yacht Club's Committee Boat for the Big Boat Series for six or seven years, so we were right in the middle of the action. I am proud to be a member of the St. Francis Yacht Club, arguably the number one yacht club in the world of sailing... period.

Here is a summary of some of my sailing success:
- 1972 – won the St. Francis Yacht Club Inaugural Inter Club Regatta in Sea Lotus with Jim Jessie on board

- 1974 with Regardless
    - won The Richard Rheem Perpetual trophy in Big Boat Series
    - won our class in the Danforth Racing Series

My 43-foot Cheoy Lee Motor Sailor used 6 or 7 times as the StFYC Committee Boat in the Big Boat Series

- 1975 – Transpac with Regardless, leading on handicap finally finished 5th

- 1979 – the "Turtle" Transpac with Regardless, finished having survived being becalmed twice

- 1980 with Zamazaan
  - won the Pan Am Clipper Cup Series for Class A Boats and top American Boat
  - won City of San Francisco trophy in Big Boat Series

- 1981 – won Transpac Class A finishing at night with Zamazaan

- 1986 Co-winner of the Jerome B. White Yachtsman of the Year. The trophy is awarded each year to that member in the club who has made the greatest contribution during the preceding calendar year to the sport of yachting. The club member thus selected is known as The St. Francis Yachtsman of the Year.

- 2018 Honorary "Lifetime Member" St. Francis Yacht Club (one of three living Honorary Members). To earn the distinction of Honorary Member at St. Francis Yacht Club, one must be nominated by the Staff Commodores and unanimously confirmed by the Board of Directors. Officially, "Honorary Members have served as distinguished yachtsmen over a span of years to the credit and honor of the St. Francis Yacht Club; who in addition shall have performed outstanding acts of service to the Club."

AMERICA'S CUP

In 1984, I was the cofounder and co-chairman of the St. Francis Yacht Club's America's Cup Syndicate, "The Golden Gate Challenge." The club had decided to put forth an effort to contest The Cup with the finals held in Perth, Australia, in 1987. Two other California yacht clubs were involved besides us, San Diego and

The St. Francis Yacht Club America's Cup press conference held on June 24, 1986. I am on the far left with Mayor Dianne Feinstein, fourth from left

Newport Beach, so it was going to be a major effort to raise funds in California. We were late getting started so we were already behind the other clubs' fundraising efforts, and we were naive enough to think we could get our effort sponsored out of Northern California. Plus, we were behind on building our own 12-meter boat, selecting the best crew, and winning enough of the qualifying races to make it to Australia. We had a lot of work to do.

We had a difficult time raising money to build the boats since we had a late entry to the program. By this time the San Diego

A celebration was held at the St. Francis Yacht Club to christian our first America's Cup boat US 49

186 • *Press On... Regardless!*

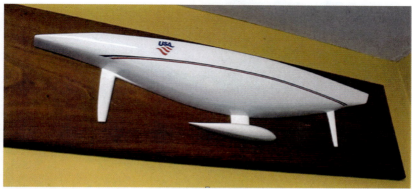

A model of the revolutionary twin-rudder hull of US 61

and New York yacht clubs had secured most of the sponsorships available in California along with the better crews. We joined forces with the Newport Beach Harbor Yacht Club since it was having the same problem. Being a St. Francis Yacht Club Board Member, I called a special members meeting, only the second such meeting in the club's history. The purpose was to raise the substantial funds needed to build the boats, and fortunately we were successful. We might have been the only club in history to raise the funds from the membership via a "special meeting." Because the boat design competition was so fierce between the syndicates, we did much of the planning in secret since any shred of our information that leaked out could help the competition. We even held many meetings at The Candy Store since no one would suspect an America's Cup discussion would take place in a land-locked building full of classic cars.

We built our first 12-meter boat (US 49) which was an "evolutionary" design, but when completed, the sea trials proved it was not fast enough. So we had a second boat built, which we called the "revolutionary" boat (US 61) and was outfitted with dual rudders, one fore and one aft. US 61 was truly revolutionary, the first such design in the world which was sort of outrageous and adventurous for the time. We contacted Alberto Caldron, a PhD from Stanford University, who was credited with designing the wings on the Boeing

Chapter 11 – Big Boat Sailing • **187**

The crew introduction at Press Day

747. When we first met at The Candy Store, he brought up the fact we had raced sports cars against each other at Buchanan Field back in 1955. We hired a second PhD, Heiner Meldner, who had earned two PhD degrees in Germany and worked as a scientist at Lawrence Livermore Laboratories (LLL). He lived in Half Moon Bay and commuted to LLL by helicopter. They both were a big help in the design of US 61.

US 61 was a faster boat and with it, we successfully made it through the elimination trials in Australia for the final races. With renowned skipper Tom Blackhaller at the helm and Paul Cayard as tactician, we succeeded in defeating the New York Yacht Club which was the first time that club had been eliminated in an America's Cup series in its 132-year history. Unfortunately, we did not make it beyond that point, but our performance brought notoriety and a bit of glory to the St. Francis Yacht Club.

A CLOSE COMPETITION

It was widely regarded in Perth that any one of the three American boats would have defeated the Aussies for the America's Cup. Unfortunately, it wasn't our boat but Dennis Connor's Stars and Stripes boat which won. We were doing so well we were told by members of Connor's crew that they were so sure we were going to beat them in trials they had purchased airline tickets to return home early.

Being part of the America's Cup effort was quite an experience, but it consumed quite a bit of my time over a four-year period. Afterwards I became a member of the Transpac Board of Directors and Chief Inspector for Northern California for any boats wanting to enter the Transpac. I summed up my feeling about what it takes to organize and execute a syndicate effort with the following words, "The America's Cup effort requires a Protraction of Patience within a Compaction of Time." This statement received a "five thumbs up" from the Scuttlebutt Sailing News Blog.

TAHOE BOAT SHOW

For some ten years, Cole European was the chief sponsor of the Lake Tahoe Wooden Boat Show. Many of our customers owned homes at Lake Tahoe and were always pleased to see us involved in charitable events. I, of course, had to have a boat and ended up owning three different Italian-built Riva boats. The last one, with two V-8 engines made it from the south end of the lake to the north shore in a very rapid time. When we gave up the Aston Martin franchise part of our dealership and kept Jaguar/Land Rover, we stopped our involvement in the show. However, the show was a worthwhile interlude every year we were involved.

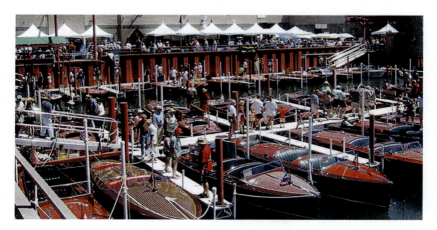

Chapter 11 – Big Boat Sailing • 189

THE ST. FRANCIS YACHT CLUB STAG CRUISE

Tinsley Island, on the San Joaquin Delta toward Stockton, has been owned by the StFYC for some 60 years. It is known as its Island Station and annually hosts the world of yachting's Stag Cruise. I've personally been on some 30 Stag Cruises, plus several visits with my family for a week or two. It is wonderfully developed and provides for several large events each year, the most heavily attend being the Stag. Five to six hundred men plus 150 to 200 yachts of all sizes and descriptions (yes, the facilities can handle it) make their way to the island beginning with a Thursday rendezvous at the SF club house. The boats navigate some 64 miles on water while some members travel in automobiles ("asphalt cruisers" as friend Kevin O'Connell would say) to spend a four-day "society of mutual addiction." It was complete with unbelievable food and drink as well as countless pertinent activities, games, sailing, lectures from yachting luminaries from all over the yachting world. Another buddy, Conn Findlay, would bring several of his racing shells and would-be rowers would attempt, with sometimes hilarious results, to reveal their inadequacies at the sport. The Saturday-night show, after a fabulous dinner listening to a live, 17-piece jazz orchestra, would always be followed by professional entertainment at the Moseley theater.

I am shown here with one of our guests on Tinsley Island, former astronaut Wally Schirra

Four kids aboard Regardless at Tinsley Island – son Rob, daughters Kimberely, Cari, and Jennifer

The seats would always fill up rapidly so Kevin, Conn, others, and I would simply hoist an entire redwood dining table seating eight and move it off to one side of the front row of seats!!

TWO SPECIAL AWARDS

The years 2018 and 2019 were very special for me due to two special awards I was presented with by two of my favorite organizations. I received the Lorin Tryon Award from the Pebble Beach Concours and an Honorary Lifetime Membership from the St. Francis Yacht Club. I never aspired to achieve such recognition and approbation as these highly regarded and voted awards convey. Yet they were thrust upon me with much celebration and praise. I feel honored as well as humbled to have been so acknowledged by my peers – my cup truly runneth over!

SPECIAL FRIENDS

WARWICK "COMMODORE" TOMPKINS

A consummate-world rank sailor. He eats, breathes, and lives sailing. As sailing master (organizing the crew and boat) aboard Regardless and later Zamazaan to victories in the StFYC's Big Boat Series and the Pan Am Clipper Cup, he proved the accuracy of his reputation and further established his position as being among the elite of the sailing world. I am fortunate to have him as a friend, and retain great respect for his intellect and sailing prowess. He also earns a living competently delivering sailing yachts – Regardless twice from Hawaii and once from Mexico – Zamazaan from Auckland, New Zealand, to Hawaii and then to San Francisco, as well as Hawaii to San Francisco. Thank you, Warwick (Commodore is a nickname), for the wonderful memories.

Chapter 11 – Big Boat Sailing • **191**

PAUL CAYARD

In the late 1970s, I loaned a new Volvo wagon (I was a Volvo dealer then) to Paul and his buddy Ken Keefe. Keefe was the son of Robert Keefe who later became a Commodore of the Saint Francis Yacht Club as had his brother Jack before him. Ken and Paul toured the United States in the Volvo with their Star boat, long regarded by the sailing world as the purest test of small boat sailing. They entered numerous regattas, making quite a name for themselves as upcoming young sailors of national stature. What an auspicious beginning – certainly a portent of greater things to come. In 1980, Paul spent his first ever night aboard a boat and his first offshore experience aboard my Zamazaan.

Myself (L) with Paul Cayard (R) on the water for a special day of sailing on the 125-foot J Boat, Endeaver, on San Francisco Bay

Since then Paul has won seven world championships in sailing, participated in two round-the-world regattas, winning one of them, has just finished an excellent term as Chairman of the Board of the Saint Francis Yacht Club (during the pandemic), been elected to the "Bay Area Sports Hall of Fame" (the only sailor so honored), been involved in several America's Cup efforts, recently finished well up in the North American Star Boat Championships (at age 62), and has been appointed as Captain of the U.S. Olympic Sailing Team!!

It is a profound personal thrill to be able to call him my friend. I must say that I have not known such intelligence and courage, not to mention the physicality, in one such charismatic individual as I see in Paul. All with a remarkably pleasant personality, carrying no airs! I look forward to great accomplishments for the U.S. Olympic Sailing Team. Press On, Paul!

JIM JESSIE

If ever there was one person I would have on a racing sailboat, it would be Jim Jessie. I first came across this great talent in 1958 at Sailboats, Inc., where I had just purchased a new Columbia 36 sloop. Jim was then a jack-of-all-trades and could handle any job the yard needed done. With a keen and sharp intellect, he impressed me to no end, and we soon became close friends. He sailed with me in absolutely every race thereafter and on all three of my boats – Sea Lotus (36-foot Columbia), Regardless (S & S designed Tartan 41), and Zamazaan (53-foot fractional rig sloop). The first was with Sea Lotus in 1972 when we won the first StFYC Inter-club regatta. Then came seven Big Boat Series regattas (we won in 1974 and 1981), two Mexican races, the Danforth Ocean Racing Series (1st in class), the Pan Am Clipper Cup International – five race series in Hawaii (1st in Class A and top American boat), three Transpacs (3rd, 5th and 1st in Class A), 1st in Class A in the StFYC Big Boat Series – the San Francisco Cup. Well, you get the picture and Jim was on board every time. An excellent cook, navigator (by sextant on the first Transpac), and helmsman, plus he could fix damn near anything aboard if needed. One side bar here, Jim was a smoker and without telling me, he decided to quit by doing the Transpac without any cigarettes aboard. Needless to say, he was a "grouch" all the way, but he quit!

KEVIN O'CONNELL

A great and close friend since 1972, now gone, Kevin was one of the brightest individuals you could ever meet. He was also the funniest man alive in my book. Quick witted with a sharp and incisive mind, he could hold his own with anyone. He was a member of the Saint Francis Yacht Club (a past Commodore) as well as the Bohemian Club. His wife Robin's family owned a houseboat at the club's delta island (Tinsley) and

Kevin O'Connell, Wally Schirra and I relax at one of the StFYC Stag Cruise events.

Chapter 11 – Big Boat Sailing • 193

I was pleased to dock my boat there countless times during the famous Stag Cruise. Kevin always had out-of-town guests staying there also and sometimes they were members of a story telling organization that would regale us with some of the funniest stories imaginable. He also had me up to the Bohemian Grove during Spring Jinx, and let me tell you that was an experience with luminaries from all walks of life as we listened to magnificent organ music emanating from the great redwood trees. Both events, the Stag Cruises and Jinx, were more than adequately supplied with gastronomic perfections, as well as libations. Kevin and his wonderful family, wife Robin and sons TD and Kevin Blair, all became close to us, as did Robin's parents Tim and Dorothy Moseley. Tim was also a past Commodore of the StFYC. Russell Head, co-founder of The Candy Store, said he thought Kevin was the funniest man he ever met after his second trip with me to the Stag Cruise.

CONN FINDLAY

A very close friend of Kevin O'Connell, Conn was very well known in the world of rowing, and not just because he stood six feet seven inches tall, or as Kevin often remarked, five foot nineteen! He was the recipient of four Olympic medals – two gold, two bronze – in rowing and sailing. He also held a Master's degree in Business Administration from Stanford where he was

A wonderful picture of two wonderful people, my wife Ellen and her father George on Windrush

the rowing coach and was later inducted into the Stanford Sports Hall of Fame. We attended that ceremony. He sailed on board with Ted Turner in the America's Cup and maintained a firm and fond relationship with Ted through the years. Conn had acquired the seemingly permanent use of a British-built rowing regatta boat named "Windrush" (after the headwaters of the Thames), a truly precious possession. The boat came from a small college in the east and had been used to evacuate the King and Queen of England during the London Blitz (he had pictures). I truly hope it finds its way to a British Marine Heritage Museum where it deserves to be. He and his dear wife, Lou, were very good friends of ours as we were neighbors along a slough at the north end of Bethel Island, not far from Tinsley Island. He had us and others out on the Delta several times where we tied off to the reeds and savored one of Lou's delectable lunches. Both Conn and Lou are gone now, but leave us with fond and enduring memories.

TOM BLACKALLER

As much sailing and racing on San Francisco Bay as I involved myself in, I certainly became aware of the prominence (deserved) of one Tom Blackaller. Regarded by the world-wide sailing community as one of the top sailors, his personage loomed large at the St. Francis Yacht Club. Largely because he committed to being our skipper for the next America's Cup Regatta in Perth, Australia, I made a commitment to become a cofounder and co-chair of the first ever syndicate, The Golden Gate Syndicate, under the aegis of the StFYC, to enter the granddaddy of international yacht racing. I then worked closely with Tom for the next four years (1984-1987) with the goal of bringing the America's Cup to the SF Bay and the StFYC.

Tom was mercurial, always on the move, always totally committed to the task and quite capable of pulling it off – which would have been a major accomplishment when one considers our late start. There were already two syndicates in California alone, soaking up much sponsor money, not to mention the crews. Nevertheless, with these deficiencies and with Tom's talent and utter determination, we very nearly carried the day in Perth, and we did dethrone the New York Yacht Club for the first time in the history of the Cup!

Because he and I shared involvement in two activities (road

racing and yachting), I always sensed a certain "simpatico" between us that provided the fuel for our rapport and lubricated our mutual enthusiasm. Because of our desperate need for funds (our syndicate was by far the least well-funded), I stayed behind in order to continue raising and providing funds. Along with Dr. Heiner Meldner (a double PhD with the Livermore Lab Group), I was in contact with Tom several times a week from my offices in The Candy Store.

Later, and with some irony, Tom and my son, Rob, were on the same George Lucas sponsored Sports 2000 road racing team. At a practice session at Sears Point International Raceway, Tom and Rob chatted for about an hour, getting to know one another and then headed out onto the track. Upon exiting the last turn, Rob saw Tom's car up against the pit wall, not moving, and Tom wasn't moving either. Rob phoned me at my dealership in Walnut Creek to tell me of the incident as the Medi-Vac helicopter lifted to take Tom to the hospital. We lost one of our stars that day.

BOB "RC" KEEFE

While finishing these writings we lost one of our stars with the passing of Bob Keefe. Friends for 50 years – one of my mentors at the StFYC – liked him immensely – a cherished relationship. Creator of the BIG BOAT SERIES – instrumental in all the many 6 meter regattas – his idea behind the wondrous model yacht displays in the club – not to forget the many domino championships with Kevin O'Connell at the Stag Cruise on Tinsley Island – he, as well as his brother Jack, both Commodores of the club – and when he spoke, and with his actions, it was with the voice of the 'SOUL' of the StFYC – truly quite remarkable; and now he is gone – but never to be forgotten. We must Press On! Goodbye, my dear friend, and thank you.

– CHAPTER ELEVEN –
PHOTO GALLERY

Our America's Cup Board participated in a television Q & A session to talk about the St. Francis Yacht Club's challenge

Ellen, myself with Cyril Magnin and Herb Caen in San Francisco to promote the America's Cup

Ellen, Cyril Magnin, daughter Jennifer, Herb Caen, and myself prior to climbing into our Cadillac to lead a parade in San Francisco to promote the America's Cup. I purchased the car from Alton Walker who founded the Pebble Beach Concours

Chapter 11 – Big Boat Sailing • **197**

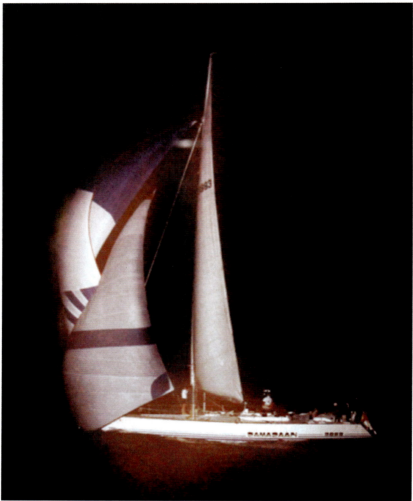
Zamazaan's first in Class A nighttime finish in the Transpac in Honolulu

1959 Stephens Flying Bridge Sedan at our weekend home on Bethel Island

Plaque from 1980 Pan Am Clipper Cup Yacht Series

Zamazaan (R) in close competition on San Francisco Bay

Hirsute me with longer hair and signature hat sometime in the 1970s

Signature exclamation mark (!) on Regardless spinnaker leading a Big Boat race on San Francisco Bay

Regardless with crew on the high side to help level the boat while running at speed

Chapter 11 – *Big Boat Sailing* • 199

The hirsute one, replete wearing his favorite hat. Manning a sheet while relaxing in Barient winch chair on the way to Manzanillo, Mexico, aboard Regardless

Left: On the cover of the St. Francis Yacht Club's magazine in July, 1985, during America's Cup (second time in Club history to have an individual on the cover)
Center: Photo of Regardless with text about the boat's upcoming defense of the San Francisco Cup
Right: Photos of Zamazaan noting winning the "Triple Crown of Sailing" on the cover of the StFYC dining room menu

31-foot Riva St. Tropez at Lake Tahoe – early use of my motto "Press On"

San Francisco Chronicle newspaper article, Class A Transpac win

Chapter 11 – Big Boat Sailing • **201**

The two StFYC America's Cup boats, US 49 and US 61 practicing on San Francisco Bay with the Golden Gate Bridge in the background shrouded in fog. This was prior to US 61 being shipped to Perth, Australia, to challenge for the 1987 America's Cup. This photo appeared in Sports Illustrated magazine and is also prominently displayed in the St. Francis Yacht Club and at my car dealership, Cole European

The crew on Regardless gave me this verse about the meaning of the phrase Press on Regardless in 1978

Herb Caen featured the StFYC beating the New York Yacht Club in the trials plus its effort to raise funds for the challenge

202 • *Press On... Regardless!*

Mayor Feinstein christens the St. Francis Yacht Club's entry, US 61, for the America's Cup Challenge at the club's press conference

Chapter 11 – Big Boat Sailing

Above: A more recent photo taken in my shop showing a few of my present car collection including Porsche, Triumph, Alfa, Jaguar, and Lotus Cortina (photo by Phil Toy)

Ellen and I flew from London to New York on the Concorde, a truly fast and exciting experience

Press On... Regardless!

– CHAPTER TWELVE –
REFLECTIONS

An American Life: is it still possible? Only if we remain "the land of the free and the home of the brave." This is, after all, a book about FREEDOM!

Now that I have reached my 91st birthday, my level of activities has narrowed somewhat from what it had been in past years. Several years ago, I showed my last car at the Pebble Beach Concours, but still enjoy attending the event and many thanks to good friend Don Williams of Blackhawk who always saves me a room next to him at the Lodge. I was pleased to be invited to the 2019 Concours, and was very honored to be presented with the prestigious Lorin Tryon Award which "recognizes an automotive enthusiast who has contributed significantly to the Pebble Beach Concours d'Elegance and the car collector world."

Even though I have reduced the number of cars in my collection, I still enjoy seeing what interesting cars come to market. I presently have a small collection (always subject to change) consisting of several different marques including Porsche, Triumph, Jaguar, Alfa, Lotus Cortina I've owned since new, Volvo, and Maserati, plus the Bentley recently purchased and last but not least, a 1913 Ford Model T Delivery Van which has been donated to The Candy Store Foundation. I am still involved with The Candy Store as Chairman Emeritus and cofounder, attending some, but not all, of the car rallies, special events, and annual Christmas party. It remains a good place to meet with car knowledgeable friends, but the COVID19 pandemic has had a dampening effect on all our activities, including the completion of this book.

I enjoy recounting experiences from my past to clubs of auto enthusiasts. I made a presentation to a large group at the monthly meeting of the Lunch Bunch – a monthly lunch meeting of automobile enthusiasts near San Francisco – about my personal background and sports car racing days. I am scheduled to return for a second presentation to this group which will cover my career in selling cars, big boat sailing, Pebble Beach, and collecting cars. Speaking of cars, I remain actively involved with my Jaguar/Land Rover dealership in Walnut Creek. This has been my sole dealership since the early 1990s and as of this year (2023), I will have been in the automobile business for 60 years as a dealer. I have rather enjoyed being an individually owned, independent dealership when all the dealerships around me are owned by corporations or large family syndicates. We have grown to become the number one Jaguar/Land Rover dealership in sales and service in Northern California. This has been a very satisfying and ongoing experience.

This next group of stories are recollections of other fun events in my past that don't necessarily fit into one of the previous chapters. They are not in chronological order, but listed here as I recalled them during the course of writing the book.

THE CONCORDE

Returning from one of our many trips abroad to England and Europe, Ellen and I needed to be in New York for daughter Cari's wedding. What an opportunity (as well as an excuse) to fly on the Concorde! Arriving at the terminal (after being relieved of an impressive sum for tickets), we boarded the aircraft from the second floor. This was necessary because the delta wing aircraft required very long landing gear to keep the fuselage from touching the runway on takeoff and landing. In order to slow the aircraft from such great speed in flight, the delta wing had to be presented to the friction of the air in order to land. Of course, it was also necessary to lower about 20 feet of the articulated nose downward so the pilots could see the runway!!

We were seated in the fourth row (to starboard), then we waited and waited with the rows in front of us being empty. I said to Ellen, "I'll bet we are waiting for royalty"... low and behold, Prince Andrew, Sarah Ferguson, their two daughters, plus two others boarded! Immediately behind me sat actor-director Ron Howard, so we considered ourselves quite fortunate to be in such impressive company.

Ever been shot out of a cannon? Let me tell you, we have! With a roar to be remembered, the Super Sonic Transport (SST) left Heathrow Airport so fast we were at 60,000 feet before we could even sit up straight in our seats. An LED screen overhead indicated the altitude, speed (some mach 1.3 or 1000 mph), outside temperature (which was too cold to remember) and other data. Through the small window we could see earth's curvature. After following Sarah to the "loo" (we shared a nod), we began to make our descent for landing. Well out to sea, the throttles backed down and the plane rose upward to present the delta wing to the air in order to slow on our approach for landing. The nose dropped down 20 feet or so and pivoted down so the pilots could see the ground. Miraculously, or so it seemed, we landed on the "stilts" and taxied to the second story of the terminal. With the Concorde averaging 1,250 mph, our flying time from London to New York was just under three hours...what a ride!!

VOLVO & TENNIS

In a previous chapter, I mentioned I played tennis in high school as the number two on our singles team. We won two city championships, plus I made it to the state doubles quarter finals one year and semi-finals the next year. I did not play much in college or the succeeding years, but had an opportunity to get reacquainted with the sport in 1975. The occasion was a gathering of the National Volvo Dealers Group in Hawaii. One of the highlights of the convention was a tennis tournament sponsored by Sports Illustrated which I entered in the doubles team category.

Ellen and I flew over a week or two early so I could find a partner and get in some practice before the tournament. My initial partner decided he didn't want to play, so I looked around for another and luckily found a great player from another San Francisco area dealer. He was a super "poacher," or net player, and we won all our matches to advance to the finals.

Chapter 12 – Reflections • 207

We ran up against a really good team of Jim Bish, another Volvo dealer, and his girlfriend who was as good as he. Bish's practice partner was the famous player Pedro Rodrigues. However, we prevailed to win the doubles group. The trophy sits in the display case at the Walnut Creek dealership.

ASTON MARTIN

In 1985, I received an invitation from Victor Gauntlet, the Chairman of Aston Martin (which we sold through our dealership). The invitation was for both Ellen and me to fly to England to attend a meeting of Aston dealers from all over the world. However, she did not want to go since the U.S. was bombing Libya using aircraft based in England. Victor was very persuasive and convinced her to attend, so we flew to London. Of course, the first things Ellen sees upon landing are armored vehicles and armed soldiers on the tarmac at Heathrow Airport. She was thrilled!

The gathering was held at Brocket Hall, one of England's best-known estates, where we stayed in a wonderful corner room and had a fabulous dinner in a large hall. We sat across from Victor and Lord Brocket, but little did I know at the time, Lord Brocket had buried six or eight of his valuable Ferraris and Maseratis on the

Portrait of Brocket Hall presented to Ellen and me from Charles Brocket – 1986

estate to collect the insurance money for them. He was discovered and later served time for his escapades.

Mrs. Brocket was an American and she requested I sit next to her at dinner since I reminded her of the American actor Robert Wagner, who had recently filmed a movie at the estate. The event and dinner were first class, and we had a wonderful time.

Victor had also arranged for tickets to one of the top plays (Andrew Lloyd Webber's Starlight Express) in London's theater district in the West End. He chartered a fancy bus to chauffeur us to the play then afterwards, we were treated to a catered dinner on the bus of… fish and chips at midnight! The whole trip was terrific and interesting.

Many months afterwards on another trip to the UK, Ellen and I were having dinner with Victor in London. Earlier in the day, Victor had sold his share in Aston Martin to the Ford Motor Company, but he could not tell us about the deal due to a non-disclosure agreement he had signed.

GOLF

My interest in this sport was due to Ellen's father, George Koernig, who was an avid golfer and a wonderful human being. He had a degree in Mechanical Engineering, graduated Summa Cum Laude at the University of Colorado, then worked for

With my father-in-law, George Koernig

General Electric his entire career as a Sales Engineer. One of his accomplishments was designing and supervising the construction of the Morro Bay electrical generation power plant.

I remember he shot a round of 93 on his 93rd birthday, a nice score at any age. Even though I had played a few rounds of golf in the mid-1960s, it wasn't until about fifteen years later that my father-in-law and I started to play on a regular basis. He joined the golf club at Crystal Springs where I was a member and we played there for 25 years. We also played at Pebble Beach a few times, Quail Lodge, Bethel Island, Princeville (Kauai), and many other courses.

After Ellen and I bought a condominium in Princeville that, of course, had two golf courses, George and I played there several times. Back home I played in several local club-to-club tournaments and had three closest-to-the-pin shots in those events and birdied all three. At one point I had an NCGA Handicap of 10.4. In all, Ellen's father and I played together for 25 or 30 years, but I haven't picked up a club since 2010 after I had my hip replaced.

I also played many, many rounds of golf with Wayne Babcock, a passionate and consummate player. Wayne is the General Manager and partner of my car dealership, Cole European. Whenever Jaguar or Rover held a dealer meeting around the U.S. and Mexico, Wayne and I would take our golf clubs and play as many rounds as possible.

DEL BEGG

Del was from Kalispell, Montana, and was my CPA from 1955 until his passing in the late 1990s. He was one of the brightest individuals I have ever known, becoming a confidante and close friend. Everything I know about the accounting side of business I learned from him. With his curmudgeonly like demeanor, supplemented by a mid-America honesty that permeated his intellectually gifted personality, I was blessed to have him in my corner. I think fondly of him often with a quiet recognition of profound appreciation for his wisdom and friendship.

After Del passed away, I worked with his son, and then ten years ago, I became a client of Elliot Stein CPA, who is licensed in five states and more than equal to the tasks that I bring to him.

A SPECIAL VISITOR

Ever heard of Elizabeth Taylor? Well, turns out her latest man-friend at the time in the mid-1980s was a best friend of a Candy Store member who I knew quite well, and with whom I played a lot of golf. Elizabeth and friend were staying at my friend's house and came to a costume party at The Candy Store. Coincidentally, her man-friend and I happened to be in similar outfits dressed as gangsters, so we hit it off quite well. Ellen was seated next to Elizabeth for dinner, and she truly enjoyed the memorable moment! When they arrived home after the party, Elizabeth received a phone call from Roddy McDowell with the news that Richard Burton had died.

JACQUES PEPIN

Ellen, as those who know her are aware, is an excellent cook. She befriended one Charlotte Coombs who taught at a Draegers (Supermarket) Cooking School (Ellen continues to this day to use her recipes), and Charlotte moved into our basement apartment for a year or so. One day, we were told by Charlotte that Jacques Pepin had visited her and it turned out she was a student of his. Years later at a Jaguar dealer soiree at the Smithsonian, I met up with him, and said hello from Charlotte, much to his surprise of course.

BOB THOMAS – THE BAHAMAS

In 1977, Ellen and I were up at Tinsley Island which, as you recall, is owned by the St. Francis Yacht Club. We had the Tartan 41 sailboat docked there and were enjoying a short vacation. Ellen was pregnant with our forthcoming daughter Jennifer, so she was not very comfortable in the high daytime temperatures of the Delta. Our only way to cool our environment was to get a block of ice from a big ice machine and carry it back to the boat. I would put it in a stainless-steel bowl and put an electric fan behind for a bit of relief from the heat.

One evening a big, diesel-powered motor yacht, 65-footer, docked close enough to us that it thankfully blocked the sun. I didn't pay too much attention to the boat until early evening when the other boat started up his electric generator for his air conditioning unit. Under the club rules, this was not allowed. I went over to the boat and knocked on the hull hoping to attract the folks inside. A fellow came out and I said, "Sir you have to realize you can't run a generator after a certain time." He replied, "I need to run the generator so my air conditioning will work. Why don't you come aboard so we can talk about it?"

Ellen and I went aboard and were served drinks (Rusty Nails) while we engaged in conversation in the air-conditioned room. He introduced himself and his lady friend who were on the boat's maiden voyage from Southern California. Turns out this was Bob Thomas, a Wharton graduate and the retiring founder and chairman of Tulsa, Oklahoma, based MAPCO, Mid-America Pipeline Company, a darling of Wall Street. They stayed about a week, and we became friends and spent a fair about of time with them during the stay. Ever since that initial meeting which started with me knocking on the side of his boat, we sent each other knock knock cards to keep us entertained.

Two years later, I received a call from Bob who was now in Florida, having taken his boat through the Panama Canal to Ft. Lauderdale. He asked if Ellen and I would like to join them on the boat (named Seabird) on a trip to spend some time in the Bahamas. We readily agreed, flew to Florida, met Bob and his lady Kay, boarded Seabird, and headed out. We went to Cat Key first then over to the Bahamas where we heard a hurricane was possibly coming our way. So, we headed for the shelter of Lyford Key Marina, a members-only facility. Bob was very well connected and counted among his friends Malcom Forbes Sr. and Oral Roberts, so we were there as guests of another of Bob Thomas' friends.

We tied up to a 90' berth and spoke with the harbormaster who recommended we secure the boat with an emergency anchor which was on board. We used about a dozen lines to "suspend" the boat between the pilings. To further prepare the boat, Bob and I either removed or secured everything topside that could be damaged or blown away in the high winds. Unfortunately, Bob fell and cracked a few ribs, so I had to press on to finish the job.

The Category 1 hurricane did move through the area, but we only encountered one problem – the wind pulled the clear plastic curtain away from the rear deck attachment points, all 24 feet of it. I was able to temporarily lash the curtain back in place until Bob could have it repaired. We had to stay an extra day or so until we could catch a plane back home. Going through the hurricane was quite an experience, NOT one I was eager to encounter again anytime soon. This was just the first boat trip with Bob, but not the last. Bob also invited us on three occasions to play in golf tournaments at his club in Palm Springs sponsored by his Homeowners' Association.

BERMUDA TO RHODE ISLAND

Our second trip with Bob and Kay was out of Ft. Lauderdale bound for the Bahamas then up to Bermuda. We departed for Bermuda and headed right for the middle of the Bermuda Triangle. About an hour out, we were confronted by a U.S. Coast Guard Cutter and asked to "hove to and prepare to be boarded." They put a dingy in the water with three or four personnel and motored over to us and came aboard...they were looking for drug runners. They asked Bob if he had any guns onboard and he acknowledged he did. They asked for permits so Bob went down below and returned with the paperwork. He had gun permits from the Mayor of Tulsa, the Governor of Oklahoma, and an official from Washington D.C. No doubt impressed with those endorsements, they thanked him and departed so we proceeded onto Bermuda.

Without question, we experienced a magnetic aberration in the Bermuda Triangle, so we had to use piloting as an alternate means of navigation. This meant using our speed and a radio direction finder (RDF) to help plot our course. However, we kept picking up a signal on a bearing which was not coming from Bermuda but from Norway!!! We kept going on that heading since we were on the null and knew where their signal was coming from (Norway). However, as we approached Bermuda, we realized the RDF was coming from a slightly different direction, so we radioed the station and were told they had moved the station to the other side of the island. I finally spotted land through the binoculars but on a different side of the boat than we expected! Later, Bob rewarded my navigational skills with a present, a serving tray which we still use.

One night while on the quay in Bermuda, we were playing poker for pennies. Bob left the table for a few moments, and I suggested stacking the deck. Kay thought it was a great idea. So, we stacked the deck and after the cards were dealt, Bob was trying to hide the fact he had a great hand, a Royal Flush or similar, but there was no reaction. He laid down his cards and said, "I've never had a hand like this before." We told him we had stacked the deck, but he was in total denial; he couldn't believe he wasn't dealt the cards and was quite upset over the episode. He was livid and refused to believe we had played a trick on him. He eventually came around after our brow beating and saw the humor in our trick.

We stayed in Bermuda for several days before setting off for Rhode Island, a trip of about three days. We were in the shipping channel near Long Island looking for a buoy in heavy fog at night. Having slowed the boat speed to few knots, I was standing on the bow, and I could hear the buoy's bell ringing when it appeared right in front of us. So after 1000 miles of open ocean, our navigation effort was right on the money.

We were able to get into Newport Harbor, but it was at night and there were lots of small boats tied up to buoys. Where were we going to tie up? Suddenly a fellow in a small boat showed up and said to follow him. He led us to a dock where we tied up. When we woke up in the morning, there was a restaurant right across the dock from our boat and next to the Manchester Boat Works, home of the America's Cup. We ended up eating Maine lobster there – it was so good that one day we had it for breakfast, lunch, and dinner.

We were having lunch one day and Kay said, "This is very interesting. Ellen, you've been married once, I've been married twice and the boys each have been married three times." Bob quickly replied "four," which was a big surprise to Kay, and this was their honeymoon!

After our arrival in Rhode Island, we traveled with Bob and Kay to Boston's Logan Airport. There we took a relaxing flight on a private jet to Tulsa and finished the day at dinner as guests of

Bob and Kay. Bob also took us to the exclusive South Hills Golf Club in Tulsa where his locker was next to Oral Roberts. Bob was very well connected. He also introduced us to a new cocktail, the "Brandy Ice" which was made with brandy and ice cream. After a few of these delicious drinks, you feel no pain!! Ellen obtained the recipe from the golf club so we were able to enjoy the drink at home... however, beware, they are addictive!

SAN FRANCISCO TO ALASKA

The next year, we left San Francisco on Bob Thomas' boat, but the weather was too heavy, so we returned. A week or two later the weather had calmed so we headed out again. Up near the Columbia River, the tides were something else and pushed us about half a mile out to sea. We made it up to Seattle to a nice harbor facility where we stayed for few days, and then headed up into Canada on our way to Alaska. However, when we stopped at the border crossing, the customs officer wouldn't let us in since we had potatoes on board. Kay said, "What? They aren't going to take my potatoes. Turn the boat around and let's anchor somewhere." We did and she made us German Potato Salad which we ate. We returned to the border crossing and told the inspector, we don't have the potatoes anymore, we ate them! If you haven't already guessed it, Kay was a real pistol.

We crossed into Canadian waters and headed way up the coast near the Malaspina Straights when I spotted a ketch coming out of a side river that looked familiar as it got closer. Bob's boat, as you recall, was named Seabird and the other boat had the same name. Turns out it was owned by a St. Francis Yacht Club member, Bill Birdsey, who had crewed for me on the Committee boat during the Big Boat Race Series. What are the odds of us meeting a StFYC member in Canada and with both boats having the same name?

We anchored in a quiet bay and tied our boats together to spend the night. It was a bit later that we tied up at Nanaimo on Vancouver Island when I received a phone call from my Senior V.P. Curley Welch about the Jaguar dealer near our store who wanted to sell. (See Chapter Seven).

We took several more trips with Bob and his wife and always enjoyed their company and our journeys together. Bob Thomas had a full life considering all his accomplishments in the business world, his active travel schedule (both business and pleasure), his high-level government and business contacts. His was a remarkable life. He also had one other goal and that was to live longer than both his parents who made it to 100 years old. He met his goal, passing away at 101.

HAYS McCLELLAN

Hays was a past Commodore of the California Yacht Club (LA), St Francis Yacht Club (SF), and the Transpac Yacht Club, and a good friend. He asked Ellen and me to help bring Charles Corbitt's (past Commodore of the StFYC) yacht, Eagle, down the famous East Coast Intracoastal waterway to Florida. Great trip – very interesting – including running aground once in the sometimes shallow water (Hays was at the wheel!)! We had much fun with Hays and his wife!

LEON MANDEL

The name Leon Mandel is well known to any automobile enthusiast as the long-time editor of *Autoweek*, writer of books and numerous magazine articles, television show host, and his time with *Motor Trend* and *Car and Driver* magazines. But what many people might not know is Leon was a car salesman before his journalism career. In fact, Leon worked for me when I was Sales Manager at Hampton Imports. To say that Mandel was a good car salesman wouldn't be quite accurate, as in fact he was just the opposite. Mandel wrote the following in the April 1, 1985, issue of *Autoweek* along with a cover story on the Blue Train Bentley. "My Bob Cole was still running a store in Palo Alto where I worked, what's more, my Bob Cole called me into his office one bleak month when my name was last on the sales blackboard and asked me if I ever thought taking up another trade... such as gunrunning perhaps, or even journalism." And the rest as they say is history.

Mandel was frequent visitor to our suite at the Pebble Beach Concours, and also a member of "Bob's Candy Store" as he called

Jim Lowe and me and Lotus MK11 at Cotati 6-Hour Enduro, 1956

it. He gave two memorable presentations there and dropped in on occasion to say hello when he was in town. He remained a good friend and supporter for many years.

JAMES LOWE & MARION LOWE

I first met Jim and Marion at my first West Coast road race at Buchanan Field in August of 1955. I won my Triumph class race so was invited to race in the feature event. I finished in between Jim and Marion which was how I met them. The Lowes were both seasoned drivers, each racing Frazer-Nash sports cars built in the UK. Jim was also the San Francisco Region's Regional Executive and a successful businessman. We became casual friends, and I would see them at the races over the next two years. In December, 1956, the Lowes returned from the racing season grand finale, the Bahamas Speed Week, having placed an order directly with Colin Chapman of Lotus cars for two of his brand-new sports racers, the Lotus 11 LeMans and Club models.

After the cars had been received at Bill Breeze's Sports Car Center in Sausalito, they were prepared for racing and the Lowes raced their 11s at events during the first half of the year as I was racing my Triumph. In mid-summer, Jim asked me if I would co-drive with him in the Lotus in the six-hour enduro at Cotati Raceway to which I agreed. He suggested I get some "seat time" in the Lotus prior to the race since I had never driven a Lotus.

After work and on the weekends, I'd drop by Bill Breeze's Sports Car Center in Sausalito, pick up Lowe's race-prepared Lotus 11 and head off onto the back roads of Marin County to Bodega Bay and back. I'd drive for a good distance, learning how the car handled at different speeds, around corners, etc. Can you imagine being able to do something like this today? Not on your life. The practice was very useful and helped me feel comfortable in the car during the enduro where Jim and I placed fifth overall and third in class. Actually, it was fortunate we finished as high as we did since that last part of the race the gearbox was jammed in third gear while we were running in third place. So, I had to motor around at a reduced speed which dropped us down the finishing order. A respectable finish in a relatively small displacement car versus the bigger Aston Martins, Porsches, Maseratis, and AC Bristols.

SCAMMONS LAGOON

One of my more unique experiences happened in the early 1970s before I got into boating. Through a friend who knew the Director of Natural History at the San Diego Museum, I was invited on a scientific expedition to Scammons Lagoon in Baja, Mexico. We had a bunch of scientists from San Diego University on board to study the spawning grounds of the migrating gray whales. I went under the guise as a photographer with about 30 scientists and journalists aboard an 85-foot motor launch for the week-long trip.

It was a fascinating week during which we paddled rubber rafts out and got so close to the whales that we were able to touch them; they didn't pay us much attention as they had other things on their minds. I took many photographs during the week and fully enjoyed the hospitality and the interesting people on board including John Bond, founder of *Road & Track* magazine. All around it was a wonderful most unusual and edifying time.

PU'U PO'A

Ellen and I purchased a unit in the Pu'u Po'a complex on the north shore at Princeville on Kauai in 1982 which we kept for the next 20 years. We had a couple of hurricanes pass through the area and a few years after the one in 1992, I was elected as President of the Homeowners Association (HOA). There had been some problem leaks in the buildings caused by the hurricane and ineffective repair work by the contractor hired by the existing board. This arrangement wasn't working out, so the board sued the contractor since they made a mess of the job.

My mother, Jennifer, and Ellen at Lihue Airport Kauai, Hawaii 1985

Several of the other condo owners encouraged me to run for the position of HOA President. I said I would accept the position on one condition, and that was a key person had to be on the board as well, due to his knowledge and expertise. He was a bright fellow who I got along with very well and was the founder of a company in Honolulu that ran homeowners' associations throughout Hawaii. After explaining why I wanted him on the board, they agreed so I was elected President and he was also voted onto the board along with a Lutheran minister, George Spindt, who turned out to be a real gem.

I made several trips back and forth between San Francisco and Princeville to deal with this lawsuit. In the end, we won the lawsuit with the money to be paid to complete the repair. However, all was not well since another owner became a thorn in our side. He was married to an attorney who we wanted to be on the board but could not be due to a professional conflict. However, he was able to gain enough votes to take over the board. He brought in a supposed "concrete expert" who wanted to expand the lawsuit to redo the whole facility. That was not the intent of the original suit which was to repair the leak damage. In the end, we received several million dollars for winning the suit, had the damaged repaired, and moved on. I spent a couple of years working on this project which I enjoyed, but was not unhappy that my tenure as President of the HOA ended.

PHIL REILLY

I first met Phil when I joined Don Hampton's Import Cars in 1959. He was an apprentice mechanic working for my future service manager, Curley Welch, and helped to prepare the TR4 I raced for the dealership. (When I decided to purchase my second dealership, Premier Imports in 1965, I asked Curley to join me as service manager. He came on board and worked with me for three decades rising to Senior V.P. and in charge of all three parts and service departments.)

Phil Reilly left Hampton's for a stint in the military and upon his return, I met with him and his father in my office. They wanted some advice on Phil returning to the auto industry and declined my offer to work in our dealership. Instead, with Curley's and my encouragement, he decided to work on his first love of race cars and eventually went to work for Griswold's European in Berkeley. When Griswold's closed, Phil opened his own shop in Marin County called Phil Reilly & Company, along with Ross Cummings, and later Ivan Zaremba, to repair and restore classic racing cars. This shop became and still is one of the premier businesses of its kind, recognized around the world for its excellent work.

They worked on several of my cars, including restoring the ancient Duesenburg engine for the Kline board track racer! I took Phil, along with Bob Potts and Curley Welch, on the Colorado Grand with the Blue Train Bentley. Sad to say that, unexpectedly, Phil has passed away. He was a lovely and very talented individual – a fond memory for me and all who knew him.

ROAD TRIP

My involvement in the collector car world included meeting two other collectors of world renown, Bill Harrah and Bob Lee, the latter of which purchased five cars from my collection to augment his vast collection in Sparks, Nevada. I met Bob Lee through the collector car business, and he became a friend and an avid car collector with several Best of Show awards at Pebble Beach, Amelia Island, and the Quail Motorsports Gathering. He purchased several cars from my collection including an Aston Martin convertible, a Rolls Royce SS1 Tourer, the Wolf Barnato's Blower Bentley and Lagonda V-12 Gurney Nutting, a one-off roadster.

In the early 1990s, Lee invited Ellen, my daughter Jennifer, and me to stay at his Windy Water Ranch in Montana near Yellowstone National Park. We all set off in a Range Rover for our trip to Montana with a stop in Virginia City, where Ellen and I had been married.

After our stop in Virginia City, the three of us drove up north to Montana and Lee's ranch. Arriving at his ranch, I remember the main room of the ranch house – it was full of big game trophies from his hunting trips around the world, the sight of which scared the heck out of Jennifer. That night she came upstairs and slept with us. One of Lee's endeavors was a successful retail business

The moose Jennifer "wished" out of the mountains

Chapter 12 – Reflections • 221

Ellen, Jennifer, and me in Banff at Lake Louise, Canada

called Hunting World that sold all manner of outdoor and hunting goods worldwide.

From there, we drove on up to Lake Louise in Banff and finally up towards Jasper, Canada, where we came upon a group of cars stopped by the road. The attraction was a huge moose standing in a marsh having his lunch. Jennifer had wanted to see a moose on the trip, so I said, "You wished that moose out of the mountains." It was quite an eventful and fun road trip.

THE ASTON MARTIN COUPE

In the early 1990s I owned a 1950 Aston Martin DB2 coupe which I had restored in England and modified with a bigger engine. This was the first DB2 sold to a customer in the world by Aston when new. I took the car on a road tour called the Mille Autunno, an annual event organized by Martin Swig. The tour route took us up into the Sierra Nevada Mountains and as we were climbing one grade not far from Lake Tahoe, the car slowed so we pulled over just before it stopped.

1950 Aston Martin DB2 coupe

A few other cars in the rally also pulled over to see if they could provide assistance. We climbed out, opened the hood, and discovered the rotor had lost its brass tip and fallen down inside the distributor, a vital part in the ignition system. As we stood there on the side of the rode with no spare rotor and miles from any service facility, we were definitely in need of some help. Along came a water department service vehicle which pulled over to a stop. The driver got out and walked over to us, asked what the problem was and after we described the situation, he said, "I think I can fix that."

He looked down into the distributor and located the brass tip. After fishing it out with a pair of needle nose pliers, he went back to his truck, rummaged around in his toolbox and came back with some sort of glue. He applied the glue to the brass tip, held it in place until it cured, added a small self-taping screw to prevent it coming loose, then put the distributor back together. Amazingly, the car started right up and ran just fine the whole rest of the trip. Since this was before cell phones became common place, we indeed were lucky this fellow happened to drive by, or we would have been there for quite some time before help arrived.

INTERESTING NEIGHBORS

In 1985, Ellen and I moved from our home in Hillsborough to a great location in Woodside on a hill just off Highway 280 with an expansive 30-mile view of the southern Bay Area. It's a great older home built in 1916 which we still live in. Through the years we've had a couple of interesting neighbors – Shirley Temple Black and Louise Davies.

I remember one occasion when Shirley hosted a big Republican fundraiser for then Vice President George H. W. Bush who was running for president in the late 80s. About ten days prior to the fundraiser, the Secret Service began to arrive in numbers to make sure Shirley's property was fully secure. On the evening of the affair, Ellen and I drove our golf cart down the hill to her property to be involved in the proceedings. The Secret Service was watching our movements from a helicopter hovering overhead as we drove towards our gate where the Secret Service met us. After explaining we were Ms. Black's neighbors, we drove to her front door where Shirley was there to greet us. I remember I had my arm around her waist. She said, "The first time I have you over for dinner and it will cost you $2000." I responded, "Make that $4000 dollars because I brought her (Ellen)."

Shirley introduced us to Bush, which was the start of a very enjoyable evening. One of our friends was John Laxault, the brother of Paul Laxault, the ex-governor of Nevada, and a close friend of Ronald Reagan. When Bush heard this, he engaged us in quite a conversation for about 20 minutes until Shirley politely pulled him away. It was an interesting, enjoyable, and expensive evening, but totally worth it!

The next morning, I was on the throne when the telephone rings – it was Shirley calling from our gate. Not knowing it was me, she announced herself and insisted I electronically open the gate. I then greeted her at our front door, unshaven and dressed in a bathrobe. She was there with her husband, and I quickly greeted her by saying, "You caught me while I was exercising." As her husband rolled his eyes, she presented me with a bouquet of flowers which was one of the table arrangements from the preceding night's festivities.

Louise Davies is best known as the major contributor for the construction of the Davies Symphony Hall in San Francisco and key benefactor after it was completed. Her husband was Ralph K. Davies, a very successful businessman in oil (V.P. – Standard Oil) and shipping (American President Lines). They were both very philanthropic throughout their lives, primarily favoring the city of San Francisco.

Ellen and eventually I became friends with Louise (she called me Ellen's beau), and we spent time with her when visiting each other's homes. We were guests of hers on several occasions for concerts at the Davies Symphony Hall, including a dinner at the Hall's restaurant. Louise would greet a parade of localities and nabobs which made for an interesting dining experience. She was a delightful person whose company we enjoyed very much.

WORLD TRAVEL

Several years ago, the finance company I used for our dealerships invited clients, including Ellen and me, to a gathering in France near Paris. The location was rather special and a grand place for such an occasion – The Palace at Versailles. It was a wonderful opportunity to make many new acquaintances and topped off with a black tie, banquet dinner. It was an amazing trip and an unusual way to get a taste of France.

Florence, Italy with Helen & Wayne

Ellen and me in France

Chapter 12 – Reflections • 225

On a trip to England – this one to sell the Barnato Blower Bentley at a Sotheby's auction – Ellen and I took daughter Jennifer with us and as a thank you, we received Sotheby's Chairman's three prime seats for the forever-sold-out "Phantom of the Opera" (yes, the chandelier came down)! The Bentley sold and thusly made its way back to San Francisco and ultimately to Bob and Ann Lee's magnificent collection in Sparks, Nevada.

In 2001, and about one year after my vascular surgery, Ellen and I, along with my business partners and friends, Helen and Wayne Babcock (he is the General Manager of Cole European), took an extended trip to Europe. We traveled from California to New York, London, Paris, Nice, Monaco (by helicopter), Rome, Florence, Siena, Sorrento, Capri, back through Rome, London, and home. It was wonderful – just wonderful.

Above: Rome – Coliseum
Below: Rome – Tivoli Fountain

SUNDAY JAZZ SOCIETY

San Francisco radio station personality Jim Dunbar and Mike Heffernan (both Candy Store members) originated the idea of holding a jazz concert. With the abundance of musicians living in the San Francisco Bay Area, we had no problem obtaining top talent for these events. We hosted three such events at our home which were catered along with a wine service and attended by close to 100 enthusiasts – good times were had by all!

IT'S IN THE STARS

Decades ago, two friends (and amateur astrologists), asked if they could do my horoscope. They were unknown to each other, and their introspections were some 10 years apart. They both came up with the same conclusion – that my horoscope indicated evidence of a "Grand Cross."

So, out of curiosity, I went to the Internet and found the following: There is no doubt, Grand Crosses are character builders. Many, many, many successful people have Grand Crosses in their charts. They are relentless and NEVER give up, therefore, success eventually comes to them and rewards them for their patience, perseverance, and diligence. Those with a Grand Cross also know their place in the world and they recognize the challenges they face.

As they say – Press On Regardless!

– APPENDIX ONE –
ADAGES, IDIOMS, AND AXIOMS

I typed up the following two paragraphs while I was in the Air Force (1955-57) and have reread them many times since then. The importance of words, vocabulary, and language cannot be overstated. The following are highlights from one scientific study which examined this subject:

"An extensive knowledge of the exact meaning of English words accompanies outstanding success in this country more often than any other single characteristic which the Human Engineering Laboratory has been able to isolate and measure. The H.E.L. has found, by scientific testing, that these exceptional adults whose vocabularies never stop growing, no matter what their age, are the most successful people in the country: the business executives and the top names in professional fields.

Their vocabularies continued to grow because their interest in life never ceased growing; and it cannot be doubted that this attitude was one of the potent factors which contributed to their success. The only common quality that Dr. O'Connor (H.E.L.) was able to isolate in studying these thousands of successful men and women was not, surprisingly enough, any such thing as tenacity, or progressiveness, or imagination, or honesty, or ruthlessness or even luck. Dr. O'Connor found, somewhat to his astonishment, every successful person whom he tested had an unusually large vocabulary. In no other particular way were these people identical."

Ever since I chose "Press On Regardless" as my daily philosophy many years ago, I have come across several more interesting and provoking sayings I liked. Many of these were things I heard, but some were written by famous people in history. Below are the ones I particularly like:

- One can only have a few true friends, dedicated to a kind of friendship which can only be described as needing very little maintenance. It is just there, always, through anything and everything.

- Nothing in this world can take the place of persistence. Talent will not; nothing is more common than unsuccessful men with talent. Genius will not; unrewarded genius is almost a proverb. Education will not; the world is full of educated derelicts. Persistence and determination alone are omnipotent. The slogan "Press On" has solved and always will solve the problems of the human race. ~ **Calvin Coolidge**

- Do not go where the path may lead. Go instead where there is no path and leave a trail. ~ **Ralph Waldo Emerson**

- It always seemed strange to me, the things we admire in men – kindness and generosity – openness and honesty – understanding and feeling – are the concomitants of failure in our system; and those we detest – sharpness, greed, acquisitiveness, meanness, egotism, and self-interest – are the traits of success – and while men admire the quality of the first, they love the produce of the second. ~ **John Steinbeck**

- An American life: is it still possible? Only if we remain "the land of the free and the home of the brave." This is after all a book about FREEDOM!!

- The mass of men leads lives of quiet desperation. ~ **Thoreau**

- He thinks more of himself than he is capable of accomplishing.

- Perception is everything.

- That person has one year of experience fifty times.

- The two most important words in the English Language – For Effect!

- Democracy is the best form of government – if you can keep it. ~ **Benjamin Franklin**

- I don't believe in God – but feel him greatly.
  ~ **Charles Krauthammer**

- WITHOUT FREEDOM ----- NOTHING!

- The older you are – the better you were.

Appendix One – Adages, Idioms and Axioms • 229

- You make your own luck.
- The empty pocket days. ~ **Leon Mandel**
- I believe a sort of Godliness in the aggregate exists between all people.
- God is a benign intelligence. ~ **Albert Einstein**
- Busy people get things done.
- Cash is worth more than money. ~ **RBC**
- A protraction of patience within a compaction of time! The America's Cup. ~ **RBC**
- Don't let the dirty bastards get you down.
- Courage is the most important virtue. ~ **Winston Churchill**
- Go with the flow.
- He can't lead – can't follow – and won't get out of the way!
- It's amazing what you can get done if you don't need to take the credit. ~ **Ronald Reagan**
- All progress is made by unreasonable people. ~ **George Bernard Shaw**
- Above all else, to thine self be true. ~ **from William Shakespeare's Hamlet**
- Anything can happen if you just show up.
- A nation that forgets its past, has no future. ~ **Winston Churchill**
- The reasonable person adapts himself to the world, an unreasonable one persists on trying to adapt the world to himself. ~ **George Bernard Shaw**
- Moderation in all things. ~ **my father**
- He who laughs – lasts! ~ **my mother**
- Always hire someone who knows more than you.

- Pay well, give them achievable incentive, give them plenty of room, and always give 100% of the credit where it belongs.
- Life is what happens when you're planning all those other things.
- Good things happen to good people. ~ **Wayne Babcock**
- Life is either a daring adventure or nothing at all. ~ **Helen Keller**
- How can I miss you if you won't go away?
- No man is an island. ~ **John Dunne**
- Experience is the hardest kind of teacher; it gives you the test first and the lesson afterward. ~ **Oscar Wilde**
- There are three sides to every story – our side, the other side, and the side in between. ~ **RBC**
- The moral authority of individual freedom. ~ **Dr. Walter Williams**
- Let's do something, even if it's wrong! ~ **Tom Barrett**
- Profit is not a dirty word.
- Success is going from failure to failure, without loss of enthusiasm. ~ **Winston Churchill**
- These are the times that try men's souls. ~ **Thomas Paine**
- The purpose of an education is to teach you to do what you don't want to do when you don't want to do it whether you want to do it or not.
- Egalitarianism cannot be mandated. It will seek its own levels, up or down, with the human mechanisms provided for our engaging in its exercise. It is an admixture rather than a dictation of the society that describes us.
- The men of destiny do not want to be sent for, they come when they feel their time has come. They do not ask to be recognized, they declare themselves, they came like fate, they are inevitable.

- I'm not worried about dying – but I am worried about not living!! Wondering, as I am, about how this freedom challenging political malaise is going to heal itself!

- **In the be careful what you wish for department:** Imagine if the socialist movement prevails – will the migrants who are now teeming across our borders become immigrants (virtual citizens) who realize that this society is rapidly echoing the horror they left and not the "Americanism" they came to be a part of – and therefore champion a concerted, coordinated, and communal effort to join with others so disposed to once again enjoy the freedom of "Americanism" (or perhaps "USAism" is a more fitting appellation)? Food for some serious thought!

- Democracy is the worst form of government except for all those other forms that have been tried. ~ **Winston Churchill**

- Success has many followers – failure is a bastard.

- Do your own thinking – don't let others think for you.

- If you are going to fly with the eagles – best to be an eagle.

- If you say something long enough and loud enough, they'll believe you (if they are dumbed down enough).

- Bureaucracy: the unintelligent and uninformed providing the unnecessary for the uncomplicated.

- If there wasn't a God, did man create one? If there is a God, did man create, suppose, compose the narrative or is God an ethereal entity? Or does the ponderable answer reside in all of us?

- Perseverance and patience have been two guiding credos for me.

- It isn't how much money you have...it is what you do with the money you have. ~ **RBC**

- Never get so busy making a living that you forget to make a life.

- It's never money – it's always people.
- No good deed will go unpunished.

– APPENDIX TWO –
TIME LINE

1932   - Born in Evanston, Illinois

1938   - Began attending school in Minneapolis

1948   - Purchased first car for $50,
a 1931 Pontiac Split Head Six

1951   - Graduated from high school and
enrolled at University of Minnesota

1953   - Purchased an MG-TD
- Joined the Air Force ROTC Program
- Joined Phi Gamma Delta fraternity

1955   - Graduated from University of Minnesota
majored in Psychology
- Received Air Force Commission and assigned to San Francisco as Public Relations Officer
- Bought a Triumph TR2
- Entered first SCCA events (Willits, Buchanan Field)
- Worked on Fireboid Project at SAC HQ in Omaha
- President of first Dale Carnegie Sales Course in San Francisco

1956   - Raced full SF Region SCCA schedule in two Triumphs with support from Rusty Hyde

1957   - Mid-year, returned to University of Minnesota for an advanced degree,
but was coaxed back to San Francisco by Kjell Qvale
- Took job with British Motors in Advertising and PR plus Assistant Regional Executive SF Region SCCA, Head of Press and Public Relations
- Involved in bring Laguna Seca Raceway to reality, then raced in the first event, Nov. 10, 1957

234 • *Press On... Regardless!*

1959	- Left BMCD to work as Sales Manager for Don Hampton Motors
1962	- Triumph TR4 introduced, won many races in this model
1963	- Acquired first car dealership in San Bruno, Calif. - Member of Triumph Factory Sebring 12 Hour Team
1965	- Acquired second dealership, Premier Imports in San Carlos - Retired from racing; acquired sailboat, 26 ft. Columbia followed by a 36 ft Columbia
1966	- Opened third store in San Mateo also called Premier Imports
1970	- Opened Volvo store in Burlingame, sold San Bruno store, relocated existing store to larger store in San Carlos
1971	- Moved into a waterfront townhouse in Sausalito with Ellen
1972	- Joined the St. Francis Yacht Club
1973	- Married Ellen and purchased a home in Hillsborough
1974	- Bought Sparkman & Stephens Tartan 41 sloop rig boat; won class in the San Francisco Bay Big Boat Series and first place in the first intra-club race they ever had
1975	- Transpac finished 5th overall and 3rd in class with Regardless
1978	- Started The Candy Store with cofounder Russ Head

1979 - Bought 53 ft. Bruce Farr designed
fractional rig "Zamazaan" in Auckland, New Zealand
- Finished "Turtle" Transpac race in Regardless
- Vice-President of Volvo Dealers Council
- Founder and President of the
Bay Area Volvo Dealers Association

1980 - Won class A in Pan Am Clipper Series;
won class A in Transpac and
San Francisco Big Boat Series

1981 - Won class A in Transpac race, Pan Am Clipper Series
and Big Boat Series in San Francisco Bay

1982 - Acquired Jaguar dealership and store in Burlingame
- Moved The Candy Store
to present location in Burlingame

1983 - Co-Chairman of the St. Francis Yacht Club
America's Cup Syndicate
StFYC Member Club Board of Directors
- Cofounder and Chairman of the Executive Committee
America's Cup Golden Gate Challenge

1987 - Acquired Oakland/Walnut Creek Jaguar dealership
- Closed San Carlos store,
sold Burlingame Saab store to Kjell Qvale
- Moved Jaguar to Walnut Creek,
kept a service store in Burlingame
- Opened Cole Motor Classics in Burlingame
- Began buying and selling classic and exotic cars,
continued collecting cars including Jaguar, Bentley,
Squire, Rolls Royce, Alfa Romeo, Duesenberg, etc.
- Continued entering cars at Pebble Beach Concours
- Unable to attend America's Cup in Perth
due to fundraising

1989 - Bought 1910 Kline-Duesenberg
Raced twice at Monterey Historics. DNS first year, finished third out of 27 racers in 1990
- Won award for Best Pre-war Car at Laguna Seca
- Won "Pebble Beach Cup" at the Concours

early 1990s - Sold Burlingame property and Volvo franchise, closed Burlingame Jaguar Service store after two years
- Became a regular entrant at Pebble Beach and eventually became a class judge which lasted 15 years
- Joined Steering Committee (now called the Advisory Board) for Pebble Beach Concours

2011 - Built new 30-stall service department in Walnut Creek not far from main dealership location

2014 - Constructed new Jaguar/Land Rover Sales facility in Walnut Creek
- Honorary Judge at Hillsborough Concours

2015 - Established Bob Cole Award for "Best British Car" at Hillsborough Concours

2018 - Awarded Honorary Lifetime membership in St. Francis Yacht Club

2019 - Received the Lorin Tryon Award at Pebble Beach

2019 -present - Brought <u>Press On Regardless</u> to fruition

Appendix Two – Time Line • **237**

MANY THANKS

To the many wonderful friends you've met in these writings (several now gone) – as well as the many outstanding friends who I've unintentionally omitted – my many thanks. They are:

- Tim McGrane, CEO of M1 Concourse in Pontiac, Michigan – a mega, multifaceted facility designated to all forms of motorsports. Previously as GM at Laguna Seca, he delved into the archives and learned of my involvements in its origins in 1957. He then asked Gary and me to write an article which appeared in the 2019 Rolex Monterey Motorsports Reunion Program – ergo, the genesis of this book! How did we meet? When he was with Don Williams at Blackhawk!

- To Bruce and Spencer Trenery of Fantasy Junction for encouraging my collaboration with Gary Horstkorta in producing this book.

- To Gary Horstkorta for his consummate knowledge and connections in motor sports and for his abilities in the computer world, as well as patience, sage advice, and indulgence with me as we spent nearly four years on this book (largely due to COVID).

- To longtime friend John Hopfenbeck for his review and captioning of all the car photos. As well as introducing us to Doris Walker in her far North habitat – 63 miles just south of the Canadian border in Idaho.

- To Doris Walker for her expertise in doing the layout for this book and coordinating with the printer. Doris was responsible for all the California Mille books after a long stint with Ken Shaff's Bay and Delta Yachtsman. Her abilities are boundless.

- To our daughter Jennifer Heinschel for her impressive abilities in editing the book. She graduated Magna Cum Laude with a Bachelor's degree in Journalism from Pepperdine University and subsequently received a full-ride scholarship for a Master's degree in Communication. She made numerable corrections to facilitate a better reading experience.

- To photographer Phil Toy for all his glorious photos in my various habitats.

- To Hawaiian photographer Phil Uhl for the Zamazaan photos which he lofted in his considerable archives.

- To my primary physician, Dr. Dale Ritzo, for guiding me through so many of life's perturbations along the some 35 years of our relationship. Also, a thank you to my cardiologist, Dr. Nellis Smith.

- To Bob Keefe, past commodore of the St. Francis Yacht Club as was his brother, Jack, and a friend of mine since we first met in 1972. To me he was and is the StFYC and I have always appreciated his friendship and comraderie. His son Ken, also a friend, maintained Zamazaan as well as crewed on her and then was heavily involved with the America's Cup effort here and in Australia. Kudos to the Keefes and a profound thank you for honoring me with their indulgence of a neophyte as an equal!

- To Ron Young whom I hired as a PR/Fund Raiser for the America's Cup in 1987. He gave it his all and his all was very good – parlaying his talent into becoming the very long time host for the mid-week Yachtsmen Luncheon at the StFYC. He is one of the most alacritous individuals I know coupled with a fine intelligence. He deserves much credit for his contributions to the StFYC.

- To Kim Livingston, the former editor for the San Francisco Chronicle and now a past Commodore of the StFYC and chronicler of the same. Plus, he was a member of our crew when we won Class A in the 1981 Transpac to Hawaii and a well-known author of many articles on yachting events nationwide. He and his wife, Lourdes, whom Ellen and I chauffeured in our Rolls Royce Phantom 5 to their wedding many years ago have remained in our fond memories ever since.

- To Harold Hughes, a friend of mine and attorney for the past 35 or so years. Because of his calm, reasoned advice, humanity, and knowledge of the law, I, as well as the dealerships, have experience very little legal activity – he remains a treasure.

- And a big thank you to all those long-timers who populate the staff at Cole European – a fitting result to the essentiality of treating people with employer-employee relationships like equals and with sincere appreciation!

- Thanks, also, to all the others so noted in these writings.

- A profound thank you to my wife, Ellen, for her seemingly bottomless patience permeated with love.

A FINAL WORD

Writing this memoir has reinforced my awareness that the three main activities I have been involved with – sports car road racing (1955-65), sailboat racing (1965-1981), and the concours car show world (1968-present) – all were in their infancies and totally amateur endeavors, and I was a participant and in leadership roles. By now, they each have metamorphosed into heavily commercial endeavors with major sponsors.

I can vividly recall getting away from road racing when "teams" started showing up with trailers, several cars, engines, wheels and tires, paid mechanics, etc., etc. I'll never forget my reaction at Laguna Seca when the Briggs Cunningham Team showed up with multiple trailers, cars, paid drivers, etc. (our boys beat them anyway).

Similar events occurred in sailboat racing and car shows. "Just look at what we have created," I often said and still do. I am not trying to arrive at a judgment here as to what has been lost or gained, just attempting to give some richness, if you will, to the amazing differences I continue to experience.

Given this vast transformation and considering the multitude of personal and physical tribulations I have endured, I feel that close adherence to my motto – Press On Regardless – has carried me greatly into the unknown reaches of old age. Early on I made a conscious decision to NOT indulge in the mega-auto dealership world, instead, I opted to follow to more personally rewarding pursuits resulting in not acquiring major franchises. I have been in business for 60 years as Press On Regardless, Inc. (DBA) Cole European without a major franchise in a very risky business!

Of course, I have had great and abiding support from my dear wife Ellen, family, and close friends. Most of all these writings are about freedom. The type and kind of freedom not found elsewhere on this planet. It takes education, work, imagination, inventiveness, courage, daring, love, compassion, and compromise to endure as a concept and thrive as a template to realize our collective success among these endeavors.

Let FREEDOM ring! PRESS ON REGARDLESS!
April, 2023

Cindy Lewis photo

     In this land of opportunity, is the moral authority of individual freedom still as available as it once was? Only if we can remain the land of the free and the home of the brave by being courageous and self-determining within the cultural struggles that are gripping our society with great impetus. "Courage is rightly the first of human qualities – because it is the quality that guarantees all the rest."
                        ~ Winston Spencer Churchill

Without freedom...
...nothing!

Press On... Regardless!

Made in the USA
Columbia, SC
30 January 2024

811c3ba2-8915-44c5-b0a2-33ff1dc30ee1R02